THE COMIC BOOK STORY OF
BASKETBALL

A FAST-BREAK HISTORY OF HOOPS

Fred Van Lente
and **Joe Cooper**

Color by Dave Swartz
Lettering by Fred Van Lente

TEN SPEED PRESS
California | New York

CONTENTS

THE
COMIC BOOK STORY OF
BASKETBALL

CHAPTER ONE
MURDER BALL

IT CAME FROM *CABIN FEVER.*

THE PHYSICAL-EDUCATION-TEACHERS-TO-BE ENROLLED AT THE YOUNG MEN'S CHRISTIAN ASSOCIATION (YMCA) INTERNATIONAL TRAINING SCHOOL IN SPRINGFIELD, MASSACHUSETTS, WERE USED TO THE ROUGH-AND-TUMBLE OF OUTDOOR ACTIVITY--RUGBY, MOSTLY.

TRAPPED INSIDE BY THE HARSH NEW ENGLAND WINTER OF DECEMBER 1891, THE YOUNG MEN STARTED TO...*ACT OUT.*

THE HEAD OF THE SCHOOL, DR. LUTHER GULICK, WAS AT HIS WITS' END--WITH THE CLASS *AND* ITS TEACHER.

BLAST IT, NAISMITH, YOU *MUST* FIND A DISTRACTION FOR THESE BOYS!

BUT, SIR-- THEY SIMPLY WON'T PLAY *DUCK, DUCK, GOOSE!*

DON'T BE *DENSE*, NAISMITH. NO NEED TO REINVENT THE *WHEEL.*

THERE'S NOTHING *NEW* UNDER THE SUN--WHATEVER *LOOKS* SO IS SIMPLY A NOVEL *COMBINATION* OF *OLDER* THINGS.

NOW GET TO *WORK*, MAN, BEFORE THOSE ROWDIES INJURE THEMSELVES-- OR *YOU!*

I WON'T LET YOU *DOWN*, SIR!

BORN IN ONTARIO IN 1861 AND AN 1888 GRADUATE OF MCGILL IN MONTREAL, *JAMES NAISMITH* CAST HIS MEMORY BACK TO HIS CANADIAN CHILDHOOD FOR INSPIRATION.

HE REMEMBERED A GAME HE AND HIS FRIENDS USED TO PLAY CALLED *DUCK-ON-THE-ROCK*, WHICH INVOLVED TRYING TO KNOCK A SMALL ROCK OFF ITS BASE WITH STONES OF YOUR OWN.

THOUGH THIS GAME--WHICH DATES TO THE *MIDDLE AGES*--DIDN'T SEEM, ON THE SURFACE, ALL THAT APPLICABLE TO HIS CURRENT SITUATION, HE *DID* FIND ONE ASPECT RATHER ATTRACTIVE, REMEMBERING:

"WHEN THE DUCK WAS THROWN IN AN ARC, *ACCURACY* WAS MORE EFFECTIVE THAN *FORCE*.

"WITH THIS GAME IN MIND, I THOUGHT THAT IF THE GOAL WERE *HORIZONTAL* INSTEAD OF VERTICAL, THE PLAYERS WOULD BE COMPELLED TO THROW THE BALL IN AN *ARC*...

"...AND *FORCE*, WHICH MADE FOR *ROUGHNESS*, WOULD BE OF *NO VALUE*."

"*ACCURACY OVER FORCE*" WAS A GOOD DESCRIPTION OF WHAT NAISMITH WAS GOING FOR-- A GAME THAT VALUED *GRACE* OVER *RAW STRENGTH*.

A VERY *VICTORIAN*, A VERY *GENTEEL* SORT OF GAME, TO CONTAIN MEN'S *BASER* INSTINCTS.

ALL RIGHT, CHUMS, GATHER 'ROUND!

WE'RE GOING TO TRY SOMETHING *NOVEL* TODAY.

HMMMPH! A NEW GAME...!

SEE THOSE TWO *PEACH BASKETS* NAILED UP AT EACH END OF THE GYM BALCONY?

WE'RE GOING TO DIVIDE UP INTO *TWO TEAMS*. THE IDEA IS TO THROW THE BALL INTO THE OPPOSING TEAM'S BASKET.

GOT IT? LET'S GO!

FWEEEEE!!

"THE BOYS BEGAN TACKLING, KICKING, AND PUNCHING IN THE CLINCHES," NAISMITH WOULD TELL A NEW YORK CITY RADIO STATION IN 1939.

"THEY ENDED UP IN A *FREE-FOR-ALL* IN THE MIDDLE OF THE GYM FLOOR."

WHEN THE DUST SETTLED, THE GAME'S FIRST-EVER *INJURY REPORT* COMPRISED MULTIPLE *BLACK EYES*, A SEPARATED SHOULDER, AND ONE PLAYER *KNOCKED OUT*.

"IT CERTAINLY WAS *MURDER*," HE REMEMBERED IN 1939.

NAISMITH REALIZED HE WAS GOING TO HAVE TO IMPOSE MORE *STRUCTURE* ON HIS UNRULY INFANT OF A GAME.

ALL RIGHT, FELLOWS...LET'S TRY THIS AGAIN...

RULES

ON DECEMBER 21, 1891, HE WAS READY TO UNVEIL THE NEW, IMPROVED GAME.

NAISMITH'S

1. The ball may be thrown in any direction with one or both hands.

2. The ball may be batted in any direction with one or both hands (never with the fist).

...or, if there was evident intent to injure the person, for the whole of the game, no substitute allowed.

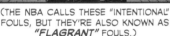

(THE NBA CALLS THESE "INTENTIONAL" FOULS, BUT THEY'RE ALSO KNOWN AS *"FLAGRANT"* FOULS.)

6. A foul is striking at the ball with the fist, violation of Rules 3 and 4, and such as described in Rule 5.

7. If either side makes three consecutive fouls, it shall count a goal for the opponents (consecutive means without the opponents in the mean time making a foul).

10. The umpire shall be judge of the men and shall note the fouls.

FWEE

11. The referee shall be judge of the ball and shall decide when the ball is in play, in bounds, to which side it belongs, and shall keep the time.

1st RULES

3. A player cannot run with the ball. The player must throw it from the spot on which he catches it.

(THOUGH *DRIBBLING* GOES *UNMENTIONED* IN THE ORIGINAL RULES, YALE UNIVERSITY'S TEAM WOULD PIONEER THE TECHNIQUE IN *1897.*)

4. The ball must be held in or between the hands; the arms or body must not be used for holding it.

5. No shouldering, holding, pushing, tripping, or striking in any way the person of an opponent shall be allowed.

FWEEEET!

The first infringement of this rule by any player shall count as a foul, the second shall disqualify him until the next goal is made...

8. A goal shall be made when the ball is thrown or batted from the grounds into the basket.

(THIS RULE LATER EVOLVED INTO ALLOWING THE FOULED PLAYER TO MAKE FREE-THROW SHOTS FROM THE FOUL LINE.)

9. When the ball goes out of bounds, it shall be thrown into the field of play by the person first touching it.

12. The time shall be two 15-minute halves, with five minutes' rest between.

13. The side making the most goals in that time shall be declared the winner.

THERE ARE A LOT OF DIFFERENCES BETWEEN THIS *FIRST* GAME AND THE MODERN ONE. BUT THE BIGGEST ONE...

...WAS THAT IT NEVER *OCCURRED* TO NAISMITH...

SK*AARREEEEEEEEEEEEE*

...TO PUNCH A *HOLE* IN THE BOTTOM OF THE *PEACH BASKET.*

WAP
WAP
WAP

SO, THE *JANITOR,* "POPS" STEBBINS, HAD TO BE SUMMONED WITH HIS *LADDER* TO FISH THE BALL OUT AFTER EACH FIELD GOAL.

WAP
WAP
WAP

C'MERE, YA LITTLE BASTICH...

LITTLE WONDER THE SCORE OF THE FIRST-EVER BASKET-BALL GAME WAS *1-0.*

THUD!

6

AN *INAUSPICIOUS* BEGINNING TO BE SURE...

SQUEAK
FWAP
SQUEAK

...BUT IT DID NOT *SLOW* THE GAME'S SPREAD DOWN *ONE BIT.*

SQUEAK

HERE! PASS IT!

SQUEAK

ELEMENTARY SCHOOL TEACHERS FROM AN ACADEMY NEXT DOOR HAPPENED BY THE YMCA GYM LATER THAT SAME WEEK.

SQUEAK
SQUEAK
FWAP

HULLO! WHAT ARE YOU FELLOWS *PLAYING?*

WE WANTED TO CALL IT *"NAISMITHBALL!"*

BUT *HE'S* TOO MODEST FOR THAT!

WELL, I ASKED POPS TO DRUM US UP SOME *BOXES* IN STORAGE TO HANG FROM THE BANNISTERS...

...BUT ALL HE COULD FIND WERE THESE *PEACH BASKETS.*

SO FOR THE MOMENT, WE'RE CALLING IT *"BASKET BALL."*

COULD YOU TEACH *US?*

WHY, I'D, UH, BE *HAPPY TO,* MAUDE...!

SO WOMEN'S BASKETBALL BEGAN LITERALLY *DAYS* AFTER THE MEN'S.

NAISMITH'S MOTIVE TO BE *HELPFUL* MAY HAVE BEEN THE INTEREST OF *MAUDE SHERMAN,* WHO WOULD BECOME *MRS.* INVENTOR-OF-BASKETBALL THREE YEARS LATER.

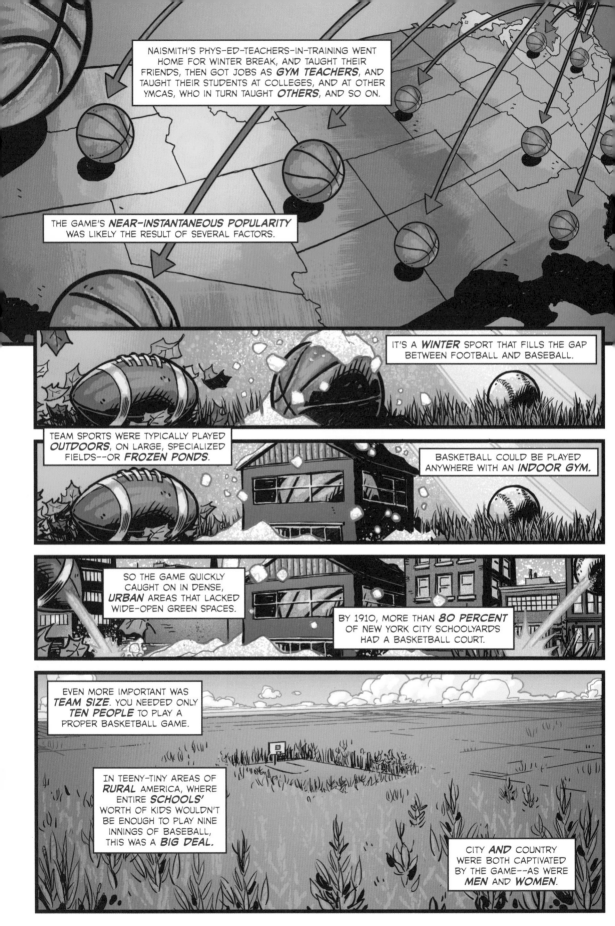

NAISMITH'S PHYS-ED-TEACHERS-IN-TRAINING WENT HOME FOR WINTER BREAK, AND TAUGHT THEIR FRIENDS, THEN GOT JOBS AS *GYM TEACHERS*, AND TAUGHT THEIR STUDENTS AT COLLEGES, AND AT OTHER YMCAS, WHO IN TURN TAUGHT *OTHERS*, AND SO ON.

THE GAME'S *NEAR-INSTANTANEOUS POPULARITY* WAS LIKELY THE RESULT OF SEVERAL FACTORS.

IT'S A *WINTER* SPORT THAT FILLS THE GAP BETWEEN FOOTBALL AND BASEBALL.

TEAM SPORTS WERE TYPICALLY PLAYED *OUTDOORS*, ON LARGE, SPECIALIZED FIELDS--OR *FROZEN PONDS*.

BASKETBALL COULD BE PLAYED ANYWHERE WITH AN *INDOOR GYM*.

SO THE GAME QUICKLY CAUGHT ON IN DENSE, *URBAN* AREAS THAT LACKED WIDE-OPEN GREEN SPACES.

BY 1910, MORE THAN *80 PERCENT* OF NEW YORK CITY SCHOOLYARDS HAD A BASKETBALL COURT.

EVEN MORE IMPORTANT WAS *TEAM SIZE*. YOU NEEDED ONLY *TEN PEOPLE* TO PLAY A PROPER BASKETBALL GAME.

IN TEENY-TINY AREAS OF *RURAL* AMERICA, WHERE ENTIRE *SCHOOLS'* WORTH OF KIDS WOULDN'T BE ENOUGH TO PLAY NINE INNINGS OF BASEBALL, THIS WAS A *BIG DEAL*.

CITY *AND* COUNTRY WERE BOTH CAPTIVATED BY THE GAME--AS WERE *MEN* AND *WOMEN*.

SMITH COLLEGE IN NORTHAMPTON, MASSACHUSETTS, WOULD HOLD THE FIRST INTRAMURAL WOMEN'S BASKETBALL GAME IN 1893.

WHEN COMPETING IN THEIR USUAL HEAVY DRESSES PROVED A *CHALLENGE*...

>GASP!<

...PLAYERS SWITCHED TO *"ATHLETIC BLOOMERS"*-- A LOOSE KIND OF A NOT-QUITE-UNDERGARMENT ALSO KNOWN AS THE *"REFORM DRESS."*

(FOR THIS REASON, *MALE SPECTATORS* WERE BARRED FROM THE FIRST YEARS OF THE WOMEN'S GAME.)

THE WOMEN WERE AS INCLINED TO *ROUGHHOUSING* AS MEN.

A UNIVERSITY OF NEVADA PLAYER GOT HER *NOSE BROKEN* WHEN SHE TOOK AN OPPONENT'S ELBOW TO THE FACE DURING A GAME AGAINST THE UNIVERSITY OF CALIFORNIA AT BERKELEY IN 1899.

"THERE WAS SOMETHING DISQUIETING IN THE GRIM AND *MURDEROUS* DETERMINATION WITH WHICH YOUNG LADIES CHASED EACH OTHER OVER THE COURT," SNIFFED THE *LOS ANGELES TIMES* IN THE EARLY TWENTIETH CENTURY.

CONCERNED CITIZENS--ALMOST ALL OF THEM WOMEN THEMSELVES-- BELIEVED BASKETBALL'S RULES NEEDED TO BE *MODIFIED* FOR FEMALE PLAY TO DISCOURAGE *"MASCULINE* BEHAVIOR."

CLARA BAER, PHYS ED INSTRUCTOR AT NEWCOMB COLLEGE IN NEW ORLEANS, WROTE TO NAISMITH ABOUT BASKETBALL AFTER SHE DISCOVERED THE NEW GAME IN A MAGAZINE.

NAISMITH INCLUDED IN HIS REPLY A ROUGH DIAGRAM SHOWING WHAT HE BELIEVED TO BE THE IDEAL *POSITIONING* FOR PLAYERS ON THE COURT.

BAER **MISUNDERSTOOD** NAISMITH'S DIAGRAM, THOUGH, THINKING THAT PLAYERS COULD NOT **MOVE** FROM THEIR **SPECIFIC** POSITIONS.

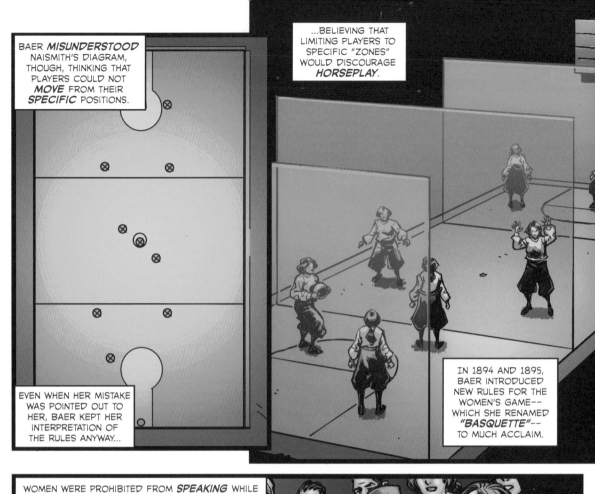

...BELIEVING THAT LIMITING PLAYERS TO SPECIFIC "ZONES" WOULD DISCOURAGE **HORSEPLAY**.

EVEN WHEN HER MISTAKE WAS POINTED OUT TO HER, BAER KEPT HER INTERPRETATION OF THE RULES ANYWAY...

IN 1894 AND 1895, BAER INTRODUCED NEW RULES FOR THE WOMEN'S GAME-- WHICH SHE RENAMED **"BASQUETTE"**-- TO MUCH ACCLAIM.

WOMEN WERE PROHIBITED FROM **SPEAKING** WHILE PLAYING TO CUT DOWN ON *"MASCULINE"* GRUNTS.

SAY, CAN YOU SEE WHAT THE **SCORE** I--

SH!

BLOCKING AND **STEALS** WERE ALSO BANNED AS **UNLADYLIKE**.

STILL, INGENIOUS GIRLS FOUND WAYS AROUND THE EXCESSIVE RESTRICTIONS TO CREATE A **DISTINCTIVE** STYLE OF WOMEN'S PLAY.

RULES BANNED WOMEN FROM BREAKING THE VERTICAL PLANE WHILE GUARDING (*JUMPING*, IN OTHER WORDS)...

...SO OPPONENTS PERFECTED **TWO-HANDED SHOTS** AND PASSES THAT **COULDN'T** BE DEFENDED AGAINST.

BASKETBALL'S POPULARITY CAME JUST IN **TIME**, BECAUSE, IN 1895, **VOLLEYBALL** WOULD BE INVENTED AT THE **SAME** SPRINGFIELD YMCA.

MANY BELIEVE THAT IF NAISMITH'S TIMING HAD BEEN JUST A LITTLE DIFFERENT, VOLLEYBALL VERY WELL COULD HAVE OVERTAKEN HOOPS AS WOMEN'S **PREEMINENT INDOOR GAME**.

THE *MEN'S* GAME ALSO STRUGGLED TO REDUCE ITS *"MURDEROUSNESS."*

WEIRDLY, THEY THOUGHT THE BEST WAY TO DO THIS WOULD BE TO LITERALLY *CAGE* IT.

IN 1896, THE FIRST *PROFESSIONAL MEN'S GAME* TOOK PLACE IN A MASONIC TEMPLE IN TRENTON, NEW JERSEY.

TO PREVENT PLAYERS FROM LAUNCHING THEMSELVES INTO THE SEATS, THE ENDLINES AND SIDELINES WERE ENCLOSED IN A TWELVE-FOOT-HIGH WIRE-MESH *FENCE.*

THE CAGE PREVENTED A LOT OF INJURIES.

SSKKSSHHH

AAGGH!!

TO *FANS.*

BY THAT TIME, POPS'S PEACH BASKETS HAD BEEN REPLACED BY *NETS*--THOUGH MANY WERE ALSO MADE OF METAL AND LOOKED LIKE SOMETHING OUT OF *MAD MAX.*

KLANG

THE REF HAD TO *LIBERATE* THE BALL BY PULLING A CORD-- THE BALL WAS THEN BROUGHT TO THE CENTER OF THE COURT FOR *ANOTHER JUMP.*

(EARLY BALLERS DIDN'T WANT TO PUT *HOLES* IN THE BOTTOM OF THE NET BECAUSE THEY WORRIED BALLS WOULD PASS THROUGH THE BASKET TOO FAST TO *SEE* AND SO NO ONE WOULD KNOW IF A GOAL WAS *SCORED* OR NOT!)

THE MEN'S GAME *BANNED* CHASING OUT-OF-BOUNDS BALLS IN 1902, AND THE WOMEN'S GAME FOLLOWED THE NEXT YEAR.

FWEEEEEEEE

BY THAT TIME, ROPE NETTING HAD MOSTLY REPLACED METAL MESH, BUT IT WAS STILL CALLED A *"CAGE."*

A LOT OF PRO TEAMS *LIKED* CAGES, AND KEPT THEM AROUND UNTIL THE 1930S.

YOU COULD *PASS* THE BALL BY BANKING IT *OFF* THE CAGE!

GOTCHA!

IF AN OFFENSIVE PLAYER GOT A LITTLE TOO CLOSE TO THE CAGE, A DEFENDER COULD GRAB IT ON EITHER SIDE, PRESSING HIM INTO THE MESH AND FORCING HIM TO MAKE A COMPROMISED JUMP SHOT.

CAGED COURTS WERE ABOUT TWO-THIRDS TODAY'S SIZE. GAME ACTION CAME CLOSE, HARD, AND FAST.

ONE-HANDED DRIBBLING WOULDN'T BE FULLY ALLOWED UNTIL 1929, AND DRIBBLING *TWO-HANDED* MADE IT HARD TO EVADE DEFENDERS.

SOME OF THE BIGGER PLAYERS SOLVED THIS PROBLEM SIMPLY BY *HEAD-BUTTING* THEIR FOES AS THEY BARRELED DOWNCOURT.

IN ONE HEATED GAME, A TWO-HANDED DRIBBLER WASN'T PAYING ENOUGH ATTENTION TO WHERE HE WAS GOING.

HE HEAD-BUTTED *HIS OWN* TEAMMATE.

THE TEAMMATE, IN TURN, HIT ANOTHER PLAYER-- AND ALL THREE WOUND UP SPRAWLED ON THE FLOOR.

BALLERS WERE ALSO KNOWN AS *"CAGERS,"* AND REVELED IN THEIR *TOUGH-GUY IMAGE.*

FLAGRANT FOULS IN THOSE DAYS WERE RARELY CALLED (OBVIOUSLY), SO FIGHTS BROKE OUT ON THE COURT ALL THE TIME.

CAGES DIDN'T JUST PROTECT FANS FROM *PLAYERS*--THEY PROTECTED PLAYERS FROM *FANS*, KEEPING VISITING TEAMS FROM GETTING COMPLETELY OVERWHELMED IN ANY BRAWL BY THE LOCAL CROWD *JOINING IN.*

IN THE *EAST*, FANS BEGAN AVOIDING EXCESSIVELY VIOLENT *CAGE BALL.*

"IN SOME CITIES OF THE NEW YORK STATE LEAGUE," A NEWSPAPER OF THE EARLY 1920S COMPLAINED, *"GLADIATORIAL COMBATS* OF THE *ANCIENT ROMANS* PALE INTO INSIGNIFICANCE COMPARED WITH THE ROWDYISM RAMPANT AMONG SOME OF THE FANS AND SOME OF THE PLAYERS.

"THE GAMES ARE NOT FIT PLACES ON SOME OCCASIONS TO TAKE A *LADY*, CERTAINLY NOT THE SORT OF CONTEST THEY SHOULD LIKE TO WITNESS."

MIDWESTERN PROS TOOK A DIFFERENT TACK, ADOPTING AMATEUR RULES THAT BANNED CAGES. TEAMS IN CITIES SUCH AS CLEVELAND, CHICAGO, DETROIT, AND FORT WAYNE THRIVED.

THE FIRST TRUE PRO LEAGUE, THE *AMERICAN BASKETBALL LEAGUE (ABL)* FORMED IN 1925 AND BANNED BOTH CAGES AND DRIBBLING, BUT HARDCORE FANS FOUND THAT TOO *TAME*. THE ABL STRUGGLED TO FIND AN AUDIENCE AND FOLDED AFTER ONLY SIX YEARS OF PLAY.

JAMES NAISMITH HAD INVENTED A GAME TO TRY TO ELIMINATE *ROUGHHOUSING*--AND *FAILED*.

BUT HE *SUCCEEDED* IN CREATING THE GREATEST *OVERNIGHT SENSATION* IN THE ANNALS OF SPORT!

CHAPTER TWO
'STORMING

INVENTED ONLY *THIRTEEN YEARS* PRIOR, BASKETBALL WAS ALREADY POPULAR AND WIDESPREAD ENOUGH THAT THE *OLYMPICS* FIRST FEATURED IT AS A MEN'S DEMONSTRATION SPORT AT THE *1904* GAMES IN ST. LOUIS.

THE AMATEUR CHAMPIONS WERE GERMAN AMERICANS FROM BUFFALO, NEW YORK, CREATIVELY NAMED *"THE BUFFALO GERMANS."*

THE GERMANS ALL GREW UP TOGETHER AND LEARNED THE GAME AT THE EAST SIDE *YMCA* ON GENESEE STREET.

AFTER THEIR BIG WIN, THE GERMANS PIONEERED *"BARNSTORMING"*-- A TERM COINED BY TOURING *THEATER TROUPES* WHO WENT FROM TOWN TO TOWN IN RAPID-FIRE FASHION, PERFORMING IN ANY BARN THAT WOULD HOST THEM.

IT WAS THE SAME CONCEPT IN SPORTS, WITH *PRO* TEAMS GOING FROM SMALL TOWN TO SMALL TOWN AND PLAYING HIGH SCHOOL CHAMPIONS OR ADULT TALENT IN EXHIBITION MATCHES.

BARNSTORMING EXPLOITED THE PREJUDICE OF EVERY SMALL TOWN IN AMERICA THAT *THEIR* "BIG FIVE" COULD BEAT ANYONE IN THE *WORLD*, IF GIVEN HALF A CHANCE.

THEY WERE WILLING, EVEN EAGER, TO PUT *MONEY DOWN* ON THIS BELIEF.

AND BARNSTORMERS WERE HAPPY TO *TAKE* THAT MONEY.

THOUGH THEY WEREN'T PARTICULARLY TALL, OR STRONG, OR FAST, THE BOYS FROM GENESEE STREET HAD BEEN PLAYING TOGETHER SINCE THEY WERE *FOURTEEN YEARS OLD*.

THEY WORKED TOGETHER EFFORT-LESSLY, WITHOUT THINKING, WITHOUT RUSHING, AS IF THEY WERE *SHARING A BRAIN*.

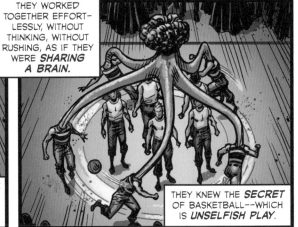

THEY KNEW THE *SECRET* OF BASKETBALL--WHICH IS *UNSELFISH PLAY*.

THE LEVEL OF COMPETITION CAN BE DEMONSTRATED BY THE GERMANS' RECORD: *792-86* OVER TWENTY-NINE SEASONS. (THAT'S A *.891* WINNING PERCENTAGE!)

IN 1908, THEY HAD A WINNING STREAK OF *111 STRAIGHT GAMES.*

IT WAS A NOT-TERRIBLE WAY TO MAKE A LIVING, IN THOSE DAYS--OVER A THREE-GAME STAND, THE TEAM WOULD CLEAR ABOUT $500 TOTAL...

...SO OTHER TEAMS FROM COMPLETELY *DIFFERENT* BACKGROUNDS BEGAN TO FOLLOW THE GERMANS' LEAD.

TWENTY-TWO-YEAR-OLD SAINT KITTS' EMIGRANT *ROBERT L. "BOB" DOUGLAS* WAS WORKING AS A HOTEL BELLHOP IN MANHATTAN WHEN A FRIEND INVITED HIM TO WATCH A GAME IN 1905.

IT WAS LOVE AT FIRST SIGHT.

"THE FATHER OF BLACK BASKETBALL" FIRST ORGANIZED SEVERAL AMATEUR TEAMS IN NEW YORK.

BUT THEN DOUGLAS GOT WIND OF A BRAND-NEW *DANCE HALL* OPENING UP IN HARLEM ON SEVENTH AVENUE BETWEEN WEST 137TH STREET AND WEST 138TH.

THE RENAISSANCE BALLROOM AND CASINO WOULD BOAST A THEATER, A BILLIARD PARLOR, SHOPS, A CHINESE RESTAURANT...

...AND, MOST *IMPORTANTLY* FROM DOUGLAS'S POINT OF VIEW, A *BALLROOM* ON ITS SECOND FLOOR.

DOUGLAS APPROACHED THE OWNERS WITH A PROPOSITION:

HE'D NAME A TEAM THE *"NEW YORK RENAISSANCE"* (RENS) TO PROMOTE THE BALLROOM, SO LONG AS THEY COULD PLAY THEIR *HOME GAMES* THERE.

BOB DOUGLAS SET ABOUT RECRUITING THE BEST BLACK PLAYERS AND COACHES HE COULD FIND--FOR THE *FIRST* PRO TEAM ENTIRELY OWNED *AND* COACHED *BY* AFRICAN AMERICANS.

FOR A NOT-CHEAP *FIFTY-FIVE-CENT* TICKET, HARLEM PATRONS PACKED THE RENAISSANCE TO WATCH ITS TITULAR TEAM SPRINT ACROSS THE COURT.

AFTERWARD, THE HOOPS AND SPECTATORS' CHAIRS WERE REMOVED SO THE CROWD COULD DANCE TO JIMMIE LUNCEFORD AND HIS ORCHESTRA.

DOUGLAS ALSO TOOK THE RENS ON THE ROAD *BARNSTORMING* IN THEIR TEAM BUS, AFFECTIONATELY NAMED *"THE BLUE GOOSE."*

GENERAL STORE

WHITES ONLY

CROSS-COUNTRY TREKS COULD BE *HARROWING ADVENTURES* FOR AFRICAN AMERICANS IN THOSE DAYS, PARTICULARLY IF THEY VENTURED INTO THE SEGREGATED *SOUTH.*

THE TEAM SOMETIMES HAD TO STAY IN THE *LOCAL JAIL* BECAUSE NO ONE ELSE WOULD RENT ROOMS TO THEM.

WHEN NO BLACK-FRIENDLY ACCOMMODATIONS COULD BE FOUND AT ALL, THE BLUE GOOSE SERVED AS HOTEL *AND* RESTAURANT!

THE RENS HAD TO RUN UP THE SCORE BY AT LEAST *TEN* EVERY GAME, BECAUSE THE WHITE OFFICIALS WOULD DO ANYTHING THEY COULD TO HELP LESSER LOCAL TEAMS CHIP AWAY AT THAT LEAD.

SEVEN HUNDRED AND EIGHT... SEVEN HUNDRED AND NINE...

ERIC ILLIDGE, DOUGLAS'S RIGHT-HAND MAN, BECAME AN EXPERT AT COUNTING HEADS IN THE STANDS.

TOO BAD-- LOW CROWD TONIGHT, I ONLY GOT 450 AT THE DOOR--

ALL DUE RESPECT, I GOT *710.*

AND I *NEVER* MISCOUNT.

YOU FEEL ME?

BARNSTORMING, OBVIOUSLY, WAS NOT FOR THE FAINT OF HEART.

19

BARNSTORMERS SPREAD NEW TECHNIQUES AND PLAYS WHEREVER THEY WENT, LIKE *JOHNNY BASKETBALL-SEEDS.*

ONE NIGHT IN THE EARLY 1930S, THE NEW YORK RENS PLAYED AN EXHIBITION GAME IN HOOPS-HAPPY *INDIANA.*

THE LOCAL STARS WEREN'T JUST A BUNCH OF HAYSEEDS, EVEN THOUGH THEIR GUARD'S NAME WAS, NO LIE, *JOHN-BOB.*

JOHN-BOB HAD BEEN BORN ON A FARM IN HALL, INDIANA, IN 1910, WITH NO INDOOR PLUMBING, NO ELECTRICITY, AND NO HEATING OTHER THAN BRICKS WARMED IN THE STOVE.

HE AND HIS THREE BROTHERS HAD LEARNED HOW TO PLAY THE GAME WITH A "BALL" (THAT WAS NOTHING MORE THAN A BALL OF RAGS) AND A TOMATO BASKET.

BUT JOHN-BOB WOULD GO ON TO LEAD HIS HIGH SCHOOL SQUAD TO THE STATE CHAMPIONSHIPS *THREE TIMES,* TAKING HOME THE CROWN IN 1927.

IN THOSE DAYS, THE BALL WAS *LEATHER,* WITH AN *INFLATED BLADDER* INSIDE, AND IT BOUNCED *CRAZILY.*

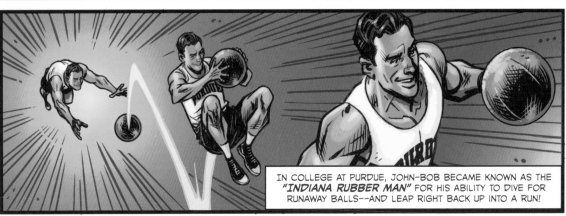

IN COLLEGE AT PURDUE, JOHN-BOB BECAME KNOWN AS THE *"INDIANA RUBBER MAN"* FOR HIS ABILITY TO DIVE FOR RUNAWAY BALLS--AND LEAP RIGHT BACK UP INTO A RUN!

HE WAS A *THREE-TIME ALL-AMERICAN*. IN 1932, HE LED THE BOILERMAKERS TO THE CHAMPIONSHIP AND WAS NAMED PLAYER OF THE YEAR.

THAT NIGHT AGAINST THE NEW YORK RENS, THOUGH, JOHN-BOB REALIZED HE HAD MET HIS MATCH.

WEE WILLIE SMITH WAS NOT SO WEE AT 6' 5", THE TALLEST PLAYER ON THE TEAM.

FATS JENKINS, REN'S CAPTAIN, WAS RIDICULOUSLY FAST AND COMBINED AN UNCANNY COURT SENSE WITH PINPOINT SHOOTING ACCURACY.

BILL YANCEY WAS UNPARALLELED AT DEFENSE--AND PLAYED *SHORTSTOP* IN THE NEGRO LEAGUES DURING BASEBALL SEASON!

PAPPY RICKS WAS SUCH A GOOD SHOOTER THAT HE'D TURN GAMES INTO RIDICULOUS DISPLAYS OF *MARKSMANSHIP.*

CHARLES "TARZAN" COOPER WAS GENERALLY CONSIDERED THE GREATEST CENTER OF HIS ERA.

AS GOOD AS THEIR *OFFENSE* WAS, THE RENS SPECIALIZED IN TOUGH, SUFFOCATING *DEFENSE*.

WHERE'D ALL THESE GUYS *COME* FROM?!

THE RENS WERE *SPECTACULARLY* SUCCESSFUL, AT ONE POINT RATTLING OFF *88 STRAIGHT WINS* DURING THE 1932-33 SEASON.

JOHN-BOB WOULD LATER SAY, "TO THIS DAY, I HAVE NEVER SEEN A TEAM PLAY BETTER *TEAM BASKETBALL*.

"THEY HAD GREAT *ATHLETES*, BUT THEY WEREN'T AS IMPRESSIVE AS THEIR *TEAM* PLAY. THE WAY THEY HANDLED AND PASSED THE BALL WAS JUST AMAZING."

AND THIS IS *JOHN WOODEN* WE'RE TALKING ABOUT, THE FIRST PERSON TO GO INTO THE HALL OF FAME AS A PLAYER *AND* AS A COACH!

WHEN HE BECAME A LEGENDARY COACH AT UCLA (MORE ON THAT LATER), WOODEN MADE RENS-STYLE *PRESSURE DEFENSE* A KEY PART OF HIS STYLE.

THE RENS' GREATEST *LOCAL* RIVALS WERE THEIR DOWNTOWN WHITE COUNTERPARTS, THE "ORIGINAL" CELTICS (OCs)-- NO RELATION TO TODAY'S BOSTON TEAM.

A CANNY PROMOTER NAMED JIM FUREY SWIPED THE NAME FROM A PREVIOUS PRO TEAM NAMED THE *"NEW YORK CELTICS"* THAT DISBANDED WHEN WORLD WAR I BROKE OUT.

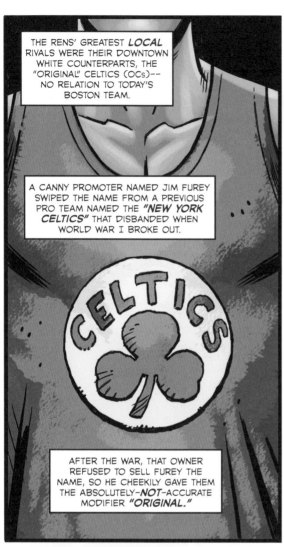

AFTER THE WAR, THAT OWNER REFUSED TO SELL FUREY THE NAME, SO HE CHEEKILY GAVE THEM THE ABSOLUTELY-*NOT*-ACCURATE MODIFIER *"ORIGINAL."*

IN THE EARLY DAYS OF PRO SPORTS, WHITE PLAYERS BOUNCED LIKE PINBALLS AMONG DIFFERENT TEAMS, JOINING WHOEVER WAS *HOT* AT THE TIME AND COULD PROVIDE THE BIGGEST SPLIT OF ANY *DOOR TAKE.*

FUREY *RETAINED* HIS PLAYERS BY GUARANTEEING THEM A SALARY--*UNHEARD OF* IN PRO SPORTS AT THAT TIME.

THE OCs WERE INNOVATORS IN THEIR OWN RIGHT IN A VARIETY OF WAYS:

THEY'RE CREDITED WITH POPULARIZING THE *GIVE-AND-GO* AND *POST-PLAY* ON OFFENSE AND DEVELOPING *BASIC ZONE DEFENSE.*

NAT HOLMAN, THEIR BEST PASSER, WAS THE FIRST PLAYER TO PERFECT THE ART OF *DRAWING A FOUL.*

AND THE OSCAR *GOES TO...*

FWEEEEE!!

"HORSE" HAGGERTY WAS THE PRO GAME'S FIRST *"ENFORCER,"* REMONSTRATING PHYSICALLY WITH OPPONENTS AND OFFICIALS ALIKE.

IN CHATTANOOGA IN 1926, A GIGANTIC DEFENDER BLOCKED THE OCs' CROSS-COURT MOVEMENT BY STANDING RIGHT AT THE TOP OF THE FOUL LANE.

"DUTCH" DEHNERT HIT ON THE IDEA OF STANDING RIGHT IN FRONT OF THIS GUARD WITH HIS BACK TO THE BASKET.

AND THEN HE PASSED THE BALL IMMEDIATELY TO A TEAMMATE TO HIS LEFT, NEUTRALIZING THIS "STANDING GUARD"...

...THEREBY INVENTING TH: *PIVOT PLA*:

24

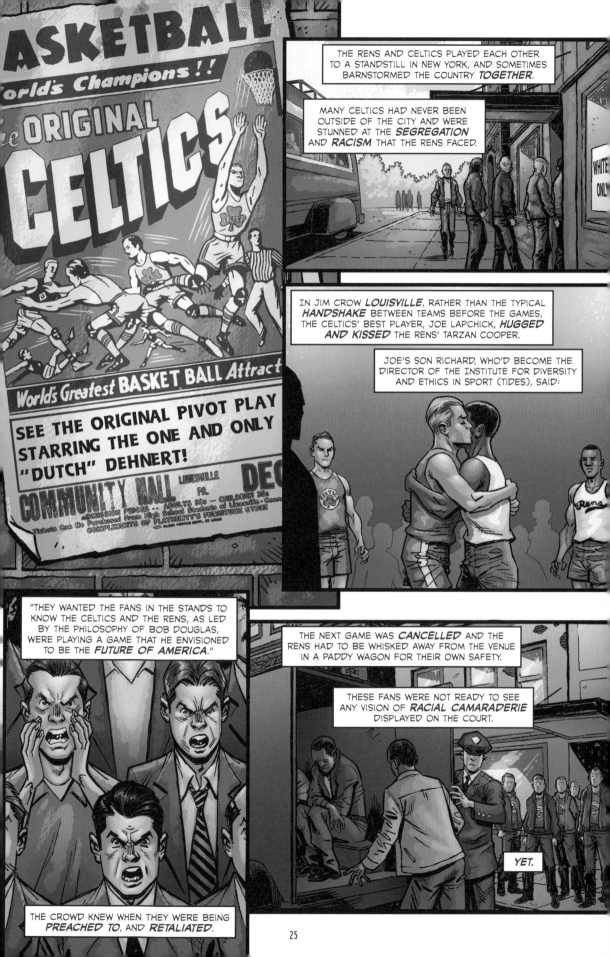

BASKETBALL World's Champions!!

The ORIGINAL CELTICS

World's Greatest BASKET BALL Attraction

SEE THE ORIGINAL PIVOT PLAY STARRING THE ONE AND ONLY "DUTCH" DEHNERT!

COMMUNITY HALL LINESVILLE PA. DEC

ADMISSION PRICES -- ADULTS 50¢ -- CHILDREN 25¢
Tickets Can Be Purchased From High School Students of Linesville-Coun...
COMPLIMENTS OF FLAHERTY'S FURNITURE STORE

THE RENS AND CELTICS PLAYED EACH OTHER TO A STANDSTILL IN NEW YORK, AND SOMETIMES BARNSTORMED THE COUNTRY *TOGETHER*.

MANY CELTICS HAD NEVER BEEN OUTSIDE OF THE CITY AND WERE STUNNED AT THE *SEGREGATION* AND *RACISM* THAT THE RENS FACED.

WHITE ONLY

IN JIM CROW *LOUISVILLE*, RATHER THAN THE TYPICAL *HANDSHAKE* BETWEEN TEAMS BEFORE THE GAMES, THE CELTICS' BEST PLAYER, JOE LAPCHICK, *HUGGED AND KISSED* THE RENS' TARZAN COOPER.

JOE'S SON RICHARD, WHO'D BECOME THE DIRECTOR OF THE INSTITUTE FOR DIVERSITY AND ETHICS IN SPORT (TIDES), SAID:

"THEY WANTED THE FANS IN THE STANDS TO KNOW THE CELTICS AND THE RENS, AS LED BY THE PHILOSOPHY OF BOB DOUGLAS, WERE PLAYING A GAME THAT HE ENVISIONED TO BE THE *FUTURE OF AMERICA*."

THE CROWD KNEW WHEN THEY WERE BEING *PREACHED TO*, AND *RETALIATED*.

THE NEXT GAME WAS *CANCELLED* AND THE RENS HAD TO BE WHISKED AWAY FROM THE VENUE IN A PADDY WAGON FOR THEIR OWN SAFETY.

THESE FANS WERE NOT READY TO SEE ANY VISION OF *RACIAL CAMARADERIE* DISPLAYED ON THE COURT.

YET.

OF COURSE, THE RENS WEREN'T THE ONLY BARNSTORMERS SUBJECTED TO RACIST ABUSE.

BOOOO!

GET THE JEW!

ORIGINAL CELTICS STAR *NAT HOLMAN* BEGAN HIS CAREER AS A NEW YORK STREET-BALL LEGEND. HE'D REMEMBER:

"JEWISH ATHLETES EXCELLED IN THE SPORTS WHICH REQUIRED *LITTLE SPACE,* BECAUSE THERE *WAS NONE* ON THE CROWDED LOWER EAST SIDE."

ONCE HE *DID* GET A BALL, NAT WOULD DRIBBLE PAST THE PICKLE BARRELS AND PUSHCARTS TO THE SEWARD PARK PLAYGROUND...

...AND SHOOT ALL DAY, DAWN TO DUSK, FROM EVERY CONCEIVABLE POSITION ON THE COURT.

NOT UNLIKE JOHN WOODEN IN RURAL INDIANA, HOLMAN AND HIS *NINE* SIBLINGS WERE SO POOR THEY USED CRUMPLED UP *GLOBES OF PAPER* INSTEAD OF A BALL.

JEWISH AMERICANS WERE THE ETHNIC GROUP MOST CLOSELY ASSOCIATED WITH BASKETBALL IN ITS EARLY DAYS.

AS SPORTSWRITER STANLEY FRANK WROTE EARLY IN THE TWENTIETH CENTURY, "MENTAL AGILITY, PERCEPTION...IMAGINATION AND SUBTLETY...

"...IF THE JEW HAD SET OUT DELIBERATELY TO INVENT A GAME WHICH INCORPORATES THOSE TRAITS *INDIGENOUS* IN HIM-- HE COULD NOT HAVE HAD A *HAPPIER INSPIRATION* THAN BASKETBALL."

MICHIGAN'S MILLENNIAL *HOUSE OF DAVID* COMMUNE FIELDED ALL-JEWISH BARNSTORMERS IN 1925.

THE MOSTLY JEWISH RESORTS IN NEW YORK'S *CATSKILL MOUNTAINS* BECAME *INCUBATORS* FOR THE GAME.

IN THE *"BORSCHT BELT BASKETBALL LEAGUE,"* HOTELS WOULD FIELD THEIR OWN TEAMS AGAINST COMPETITORS.

IN THOSE DAYS, COLLEGE PLAYERS COULD PICK UP EXTRA MONEY OVER THE SUMMER WORKING AS CATSKILLS WAITERS...UNTIL GAME TIME.

SAY...ISN'T THAT "ALL-CITY" HOLMAN?

TEENAGE *NAT HOLMAN* JOINED A TOURING TEAM AFTER BEING SPOTTED BY THE SEWARD PARK PLAYGROUND DIRECTOR. *"THE ROOSEVELT BIG FIVE"* BARNSTORMED MOUNTAIN TOWNS IN THE CATSKILLS, APPALACHIANS, AND BERKSHIRES.

HIS TEAMMATES SAID, "HE CAN PASS THE BALL THROUGH A KEYHOLE."

HE ALSO BECAME LEGENDARY FOR HIS *UNFLAPPABLE DEMEANOR.*

ONCE WHEN WALKING TO THE FOUL LINE TO MAKE A SHOT, THE CROWD SHOUTED AND HOOTED AT HIM.

HE STARED DOWN THE *OPPOSING BENCH* UNTIL THE CROWD WAS *COWED INTO SILENCE.*

THEN, *STILL* STARING AT THE BENCH, HE *MADE* THE SHOT.

NOTHING BUT *NET.*

JEWISH AMERICANS INNOVATED *OFF* THE COURT TOO.

BORN IN 1902 IN LONDON TO POLISH PARENTS, *ABRAHAM SAPERSTEIN* MOVED WITH HIS FAMILY TO A ROUGH PART OF CHICAGO KNOWN AS THE "POOR JEWS' QUARTER" WHEN HE WAS FIVE YEARS OLD.

A SMALL KID--AT 5' 3", HE IS, IN FACT, THE *SHORTEST MALE MEMBER* OF THE BASKETBALL HALL OF FAME--HE HIT THE GYM TO LEARN *BOXING* AND TO FOIL *BULLIES*.

SOON, ABE FELL IN LOVE WITH *ALL* SPORTS AND EXCELLED AT BASEBALL, BOXING, FOOTBALL, HORSE RIDING, AND--GUESS WHAT?--BASKETBALL.

AFTER SCHOOL, HE BECAME SOMETHING OF AN AIMLESS YOUNG MAN, A COLLEGE DROPOUT SLEEPING ON HIS MOTHER'S COUCH. HE GOT A JOB WITH THE *CITY* COACHING AN AMATEUR ALL-BLACK HOOPS TEAM, THE CHICAGO REDS.

ABE'S JOB BROUGHT HIM INTO CONTACT WITH CHICAGO'S ROBUST *BLACK SPORTS BUSINESS*. HE STARTED OUT BOOKING VENUES FOR A BARNSTORMING BLACK BASEBALL TEAM AND THEN GOT SIMILAR WORK FOR TRAVELING BASKETBALL TEAMS.

(AFRICAN AMERICAN TEAMS OFTEN EMPLOYED *WHITE BOOKERS* AND *ROAD MANAGERS* TO SMOOTH RELATIONS WITH THE WHITE TOWNS WHERE THEY PLAYED.)

NO DOUBT INSPIRED BY THE RENAISSANCE, WHEN THE SAVOY BALLROOM OPENED ON THE SOUTH SIDE (AKA *"CHICAGO'S HARLEM"*) IN THE FALL OF 1927, IT FIELDED THE SEMIPRO BLACK TEAM THAT USED TO CALL THE *GILES POST* ARMORY ITS HOME.

THE TEAM MOVED AFTER A FALLING OUT WITH THE POST COMMANDER OF THE EIGHTH REGIMENT. INTO THE VACUUM MOVED A NEW TEAM FOUNDED BY EX-*SAVOY FIVE* PLAYER TOMMY BROOKINS, WHO THEN HIRED *SAPERSTEIN* AS *BOOKER*.

SAPERSTEIN WAS GOOD AT HIS JOB--MAYBE A LITTLE *TOO* GOOD.

I SAW YOUR TEAM PLAY IN LOCKPORT THE OTHER NIGHT! YOU WERE GREAT!

THANKS, KID...!

LOCKPORT? I NEVER EVEN *SMELLED* LOCKPORT!

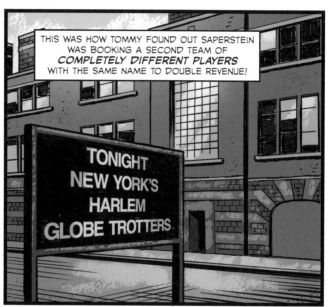

THIS WAS HOW TOMMY FOUND OUT SAPERSTEIN WAS BOOKING A SECOND TEAM OF *COMPLETELY DIFFERENT PLAYERS* WITH THE SAME NAME TO DOUBLE REVENUE!

TONIGHT NEW YORK'S HARLEM GLOBE TROTTERS

SO WE'RE TOTALLY CLEAR, HERE, THE "HARLEM" "GLOBE TROTTERS"*:

HARLEM GLOBETROTTERS

☑ NOT FROM HARLEM

☑ I DO NOT TROT GLOBE

* SPELLED AS TWO WORDS UNTIL 1947

ABE USED THE *"HARLEM"* NAME BECAUSE AS THE UNIVERSALLY RECOGNIZED HEART OF BLACK AMERICA, IT CLUED IN WHITE TOWNS TO THE RACIAL MAKE-UP OF THE TEAM *BEFORE* THEY ARRIVED, THEREBY FORESTALLING ANY POTENTIAL UNPLEASANTRIES.

HERE COMES ANOTHER *"TANK TOWN!"*

ONE OF THE FIRST GLOBE TROTTER STARS, AL "RUNT" PULLINS, CALLED THEM "TANK TOWNS" BECAUSE THEIR ONLY DISTINGUISHING FEATURES FROM A DISTANCE WERE THE *WATER TANKS* RISING UP OUT OF THE HORIZON.

LIKE THE BUFFALO GERMANS AND HARLEM RENS, THE FIRST GLOBE TROTTERS HAD ALL GROWN UP TOGETHER IN CHICAGO, AND PLAYED IN AN EASY, ALMOST UNCONSCIOUS WAY BORN OF THEIR *FAMILIARITY* WITH EACH OTHER.

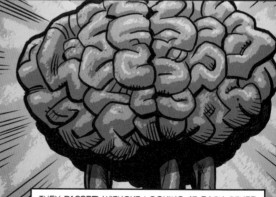

THEY PASSED WITHOUT LOOKING AT EACH OTHER AND DEMOLISHED THEIR LOCAL OPPONENTS WITH SUCH EASE THAT THE *STUNTS* FOR WHICH THEY WOULD LATER BECOME FAMOUS GREW *ORGANICALLY*...FROM *BOREDOM*.

RUNT WAS A MASTER OF THE HIDDEN-BALL TRICK.

INMAN JACKSON'S JUMPING SKILLS WERE SO GOOD, HE COULD DO A HOOK *BEHIND HIS BACK...*

...AND BLOCK AN OPPONENT'S SHOT *THROUGH* THE NET!

WHITE AUDIENCES WERE SO STUNNED AT THE GLOBE TROTTERS' FEATS OF SKILL THAT THEY OVERLOOKED THE FACT THE BLACK CHICAGOANS SPECIALIZED IN MAKING THEIR HOMETOWN *HOOPS HEROES* LOOK LIKE FOOLS.

WHILE TODAY WE'RE USED TO THINKING OF THE GLOBE TROTTERS' GAMES AS SOMETHING SCRIPTED, LIKE A *PRO WRESTLING MATCH...*

...THE GLOBE TROTTERS FIRST *EARNED THE RIGHT TO CLOWN* BY RUNNING UP RIDICULOUSLY HIGH SCORES (BY 1930S STANDARDS) AND *THEN* COASTING THE REST OF THE WAY.

》YAWN《

THEIR ACT *WORKED*--THE GLOBE TROTTERS WERE A RARE BUSINESS SUCCESS IN THE MIDDLE OF THE *GREAT DEPRESSION* AND ABE SOON BECAME QUITE WEALTHY.

RUNT *QUIT* WHEN HE DEMANDED THE PLAYERS GET MORE OF A CUT OF THE TEAM'S TAKE AND ABE *REFUSED.*

ONCE RUNT LEFT, THE *CLOWNING* BECAME MORE AND MORE A PART OF THE GLOBE TROTTERS' GAME.

THIS IS THE *BEST TEAM* I'VE EVER HAD!

AS LATER SHOW-BIZ IMPRESARIOS WOULD ALSO DISCOVER, ABE FIGURED OUT THAT THE *BRAND* OF THE GLOBE TROTTERS MEANT MORE THAN WHOEVER ACTUALLY MADE UP THE TEAM.

THIS IS THE *BEST TEAM* I'VE EVER HAD!

THIS IS THE *BEST TEAM* I'VE EVER HAD!

SAPERSTEIN WAS A MASTER OF BARNUM-ESQUE PUFFERY, AND HIS CONSTANT BOASTING IRRITATED THE AFRICAN AMERICAN PRESS.

THE TROTTERS ARE THE *"COLORED CHAMPIONS"* OF BASKETBALL!

YEAH? *PROVE* IT-- PLAY THE *RENS!*

THERE WERE INNUMERABLE REASONS FOR THE BLACK COMMUNITY TO PREFER THE *RENAISSANCE*.

UNLIKE THE TROTTERS, THEY WERE ACTUALLY *FROM* HARLEM, *BLACK-OWNED*, AND CONSTANTLY PLAYED--AND BEAT--THE BEST PRO WHITE TEAMS, NOT JUST SOME HICK TOWN'S TALLEST FIVE.

THE BLACK PRESS ALSO DENOUNCED THE GLOBE TROTTERS' *CLOWNING* AS REFLECTING *POORLY* ON THE COMMUNITY.

(THOUGH IT DOES SEEM A *LITTLE* UNFAIR TO DISMISS THE GLOBE TROTTERS AS LITTLE MORE THAN A *MINSTREL SHOW* WHEN THEIR *ENTIRE SCHTICK* WAS TO MAKE *WHITE PEOPLE* LOOK *STUPID*.)

TELLINGLY, SAPERSTEIN KEPT *THREATENING* TO PLAY THE RENS TO SETTLE THE QUESTION, BUT THEN INVENTED *EXCUSES* TO SLIP OUT OF THE CHALLENGE.

WHAT? OH...YEAH...THE *GAME*. SORRY, I FORGOT...!

FINALLY, IN 1939, THE RENS AND THE GLOBE TROTTERS WERE THE ONLY BLACK TEAMS INVITED TO CHICAGO'S *WORLD PROFESSIONAL BASKETBALL CHAMPIONSHIP* BY THE HEARST NEWSPAPERS.

"AT THE TIME, THERE WERE NO LESS THAN A *SCORE* OF PROFESSIONAL BASKETBALL TEAMS, ALL ADVERTISING THEMSELVES AS *WORLD'S CHAMPIONS*," HEARST SPORTS EDITOR EDWARD W. COCHRANE REMEMBERED IN 1941.

THE TOURNAMENT WAS INTENDED TO SETTLE THE QUESTION ONCE AND FOR ALL.

New York Renaissance

~~New York Yankees~~
(Not baseball Yankees)

~~Chicago Harmons~~

Harlem Globe Trotters

New York Renaissance

Harlem Globe Trotters

???

???

WINNER

BUT THE EVENT'S ORGANIZERS MADE SURE THAT THE ONLY TWO BLACK TEAMS WERE IN THE *SAME BRACKET* SO THERE'D BE AT LEAST ONE *WHITE* TEAM IN THE CHAMPIONSHIP GAME.

THOUGH, AS FAR AS *BLACK BASKETBALL* WAS CONCERNED, THE LONG-AWAITED GLOBE TROTTERS/RENS SHOWDOWN *WAS* THE CHAMPIONSHIP.

AFTER BEATING THEIR RESPECTIVE WHITE OPPONENTS IN EARLIER ROUNDS, THE TROTTERS AND RENS FACED EACH OTHER IN THE SEMIFINALS.

THE FABLED CONTEST, AS HAPPENS SO OFTEN IN SPORTS, TURNED OUT TO BE **ANTICLIMACTIC**.

THE RENS RAN UP AN 8-1 SCORE AT THE START, AND THE GLOBE TROTTERS WENT **FIFTEEN MINUTES** WITHOUT SCORING.

NOW THE **TROTTERS** WERE THE **LOCAL** TEAM GETTING TROUNCED BY THE **OUT-OF-TOWNERS!**

HOWEVER, IN THE SECOND HALF, THE TROTTERS MIRACULOUSLY MANAGED TO CUT THE SCORE TO 25-23...

...BUT IT WAS **TARZAN COOPER** WHO DELIVERED THE DEATHBLOW, BREAKING DOWN THE CENTER OF THE LINE AND LAYING UP THE DECISIVE 2-POINTER.

THE **REAL** HARLEM TEAM HAD BEATEN THE **FAUX** ONE, AND NO AMOUNT OF **SAPERSTEIN BLUSTER** COULD CHANGE THAT.

THE **ACTUAL** CHAMPIONSHIP GAME AGAINST THE OSHKOSH ALL-STARS DREW LESS THAN **HALF** THE FANS AS THAT SEMIFINAL!

THOSE WHO DID SHOW UP SAW THE RENS PULL OUT A 34-25 VICTORY.

BOB DOUGLAS HAD CHAMPIONSHIP JERSEYS MADE FOR HIS SQUAD-- ITS LOGO LIKELY MEANT AS A DIG AT SAPERSTEIN'S COMMON BOAST.

N.Y. RENS COLORED WORLD CHAMPIONS

BUT RENS STARTING GUARD JOHN **"BOY WONDER"** ISAACS THOUGHT IT HAD ROOM FOR IMPROVEMENT.

YOU'RE RUINING THE JACKET!

NO...

...I JUST MADE IT **REAL**.

CHAPTER THREE
NO MONEY, MO' PROBLEMS

MEANWHILE, PEOPLE KEPT TRYING TO START A **PRO BASKETBALL LEAGUE** EQUIVALENT TO MLB OR THE NFL—AND KEPT **FAILING MISERABLY.**

PART OF THE PROBLEM WITH A VIABLE **PRO** LEAGUE WAS THAT THE **AMATEUR** GAME WAS ALREADY **EVERYWHERE.**

NBL
1898-1904

ABL
1925-1931
1933-1955

MBC
1935-1936

("WHY BUY THE **COW** WHEN THE MILK IS **FREE**," AS THE SAYING GOES.)

AN ALPHABET SOUP OF AGENCIES CONTROLLED THE COLLEGE GAME EARLY ON.

THE **NIT (NATIONAL INVITATION TOURNAMENT)** WAS FOUNDED A YEAR BEFORE THE NATIONAL COLLEGIATE ATHLETIC ASSOCIATION'S (NCAA) TOURNAMENT, AND UNTIL THE MID-1950S WAS THE MORE COVETED TITLE.

AS HOST OF THE NIT **AND** NCAA TOURNEYS, NEW YORK'S **MADISON SQUARE GARDEN** BOASTED IT WAS "BASKETBALL CAPITAL OF THE WORLD."

THE **AMATEUR ATHLETIC UNION (AAU)** REGULATED NONCOLLEGIATE COMPETITIONS AND RAN (UNTIL 1978) THE UNITED STATES' **OLYMPIC** PROGRAM.

ALL THE ORGANIZATIONS TOOK IT AS GOSPEL THAT "AMATEUR" WAS EQUIVALENT TO "MAKING NO MONEY."

BUSINESSES IN SMALLER TOWNS AND CITIES SPONSORED AMATEUR *"INDUSTRIAL TEAMS"* AS AN ADVERTISING OPPORTUNITY, AND COMPETITION FOR PLAYERS WAS *INTENSE.*

ONE OF DALLAS'S *EMPLOYERS CASUALTY* INSURANCE COMPANY TYPISTS JUST *HAPPENED* TO BE THE WORLD'S MOST ACCOMPLISHED *FEMALE ATHLETE.*

MILDRED "BABE" DIDRIKSON CLAIMED SHE GOT HER NICKNAME WHEN SHE HIT FIVE HOME RUNS IN A SINGLE CHILDHOOD BASEBALL GAME...

...THOUGH HER NORWEGIAN EMIGRANT PARENTS ALWAYS SAID *"BEBE"* WAS A FAMILIAL TERM OF ENDEARMENT.

"MIGHTY MILDRED" WAS THE STAR FORWARD OF HER BEAUMONT, TEXAS, HIGH SCHOOL TEAM AT JUST 5' 5".

THE MISS ROYAL PURPLES DIDN'T KNOW WHAT LOSING WAS, WE NEVER *BELIEVED* WE'D LOSE.

AND WHEN BABE PLAYED FROM 1927-30, THEY NEVER DID.

WATCHING IN THE STANDS AS THE MISS ROYAL PURPLES TROUNCED HOUSTON HEIGHTS HIGH WAS *COLONEL MELVIN JACKSON McCOMBS,* THE DALLAS INSURANCE COMPANY'S ATHLETIC MANAGER.

BABE SCORED TWENTY-SIX POINTS AND MADE BEAUMONT THE TEXAS STATE CHAMPS.

TO NOT RUN AFOUL OF THE *AAU*, THE COLONEL GAVE BABE A JOB AS A "TYPIST."

BUT EVERYBODY KNEW HER *REAL JOB* WAS TO WIN GAMES FOR THE COMPANY'S INDUSTRIAL TEAM, THE *GOLDEN CYCLONES.* SHE MADE *$75* A MONTH WHEN HER FELLOW TYPISTS MADE ONLY *$50.*

BABE *DID* HER JOB. IN 1931, SHE LED THE CYCLONES TO THE AAU CHAMPIONSHIPS AND WAS NAMED *ALL-AMERICAN.*

I KNOW I'M NOT *PRETTY,* BUT I *DO* TRY TO BE *GRACEFUL!*

NICKNAME ASIDE, BABE WAS NO *WAIF.*

STUBBORN AND QUICK TO TAKE OFFENSE AT PERCEIVED (AND ACTUAL) SLIGHTS, SHE EMBODIED THE *"MANISHNESS"* THAT CRITICS OF FEMALE SPORTS FEARED WOULD INFECT AMERICAN WOMEN.

IN THE 1920S, AN OUTRIGHT *BAN* ON WOMEN'S SPORTS GAINED RENEWED ENERGY, AND *BASKETBALL* WAS A FAVORITE TARGET.

SOME SOCIAL REFORMERS ALSO WANTED TO BAN *MEN'S* SPORTS AS *CORRUPTIVE* AND *BRUTAL,* AND GENUINELY SOUGHT TO SPARE WOMEN THE SAME FATE.

AAAOOOOOOOooo

OTHERS SAID THAT BASKETBALL WAS TOO *TAXING* FOR WOMEN, THAT ATHLETICISM DISRUPTED THEIR *MENSTRUAL CYCLES...*

...ONE EARLY-TWENTIETH-CENTURY CRITICISM OF WOMEN'S SPORTS WAS THAT THIS WAS INDICATIVE OF THE *HYMEN SHRINKING,* AND THAT, ULTIMATELY, FEMALE ATHLETES WOULD LITERALLY *TURN INTO MEN!*

EVEN PHYSICAL EDUCATION PIONEERS WHO *SUPPORTED* WOMEN'S FITNESS IN GENERAL DENOUNCED THE *COMPETITION* INHERENT IN ORGANIZED SPORTS:

THE GREAT DESIRE TO *WIN* AND THE EXCITEMENT OF THE GAME WOULD MAKE OUR WOMEN DO SADLY *UNWOMANLY* THINGS.

(NAISMITH HALL-OF-FAMER AND SMITH COLLEGE PHYS ED PIONEER *SENDA BERENSON*)

THESE AGENTS OF PATRIARCHY WERE LARGELY WEALTHY, POLITICALLY CONNECTED *WOMEN*--IN FACT, WOMEN'S BASKETBALL HAD NO GREATER FOE THAN THE HEAD OF THE *GIRL SCOUTS OF AMERICA*, FUTURE FIRST LADY OF THE UNITED STATES *LOU HENRY HOOVER*.

SHE HELPED FOUND THE *WOMEN'S DIVISION* OF THE NATIONAL AMATEUR ATHLETIC FOUNDATION (NAAF).

HMMPH!

AN AVID BICYCLIST HERSELF, HOOVER WASN'T AGAINST *SPORTS* SO MUCH AS SHE OPPOSED *COMPETITION* AS "UNLADYLIKE."

THE WOMEN'S DIVISON BANNED *SELLING TICKETS* TO WOMEN'S GAMES, *MALE COACHES* ON FEMALE TEAMS, *TRAVEL* TO AWAY GAMES, EXTRAMURAL COMPETITION, AND *PUBLICIZING* WOMEN'S MATCHES AS DETRIMENTAL TO FEMALE MORALITY.

NO GIRLS ALLOWED

HIGH SCHOOL TOURNAMENTS FOR GIRLS SHUT DOWN ALL OVER THE COUNTRY.

IN THE HALLS OF AMERICA'S SCHOOLS, SIGNS BEGAN APPEARING.

DON'T BE A MUSCLE MOLL

AS THE TOMBOYISH FACE OF WOMEN'S SPORTS, *BABE DIDRIKSON* WAS HOUNDED RELENTLESSLY.

THE AAU RATHER *TRANSPARENTLY* ADDED A RULE THAT *FEMALE* PLAYERS COULD NOT BE REFERRED TO BY *NICKNAMES*.

I AM SORRY TO FOIL YOUR PLANS, BUT MY BIRTHRIGHT NAME IS OFFICIALLY *MILDRED BABE DIDRIKSON*. BABE IS *NOT* A NICKNAME.

THE FIRST ONE OF YOU GUYS REFERRING TO ME IN HIS STORIES AS *MILDRED* INSTEAD OF *BABE* IS GOING TO GET A PUNCH IN THE NOSE.

GULP! OKAY, YOU *GOT* IT MIL--*BABE*!

PRESS

Birth Certificate "BABE"

THE APEX--OR *NADIR*--OF WOMEN'S DIVISION INTERFERENCE CAME WHEN HOOVER'S GROUP BEGAN PROTESTING WOMEN'S INCLUSION IN THE *OLYMPIC GAMES*, STARTING IN 1929 AS *"OFFER[ING] OPPORTUNITY FOR THE EXPLOITATION OF GIRLS AND WOMEN."*

THE AMERICAN OLYMPIC COMMITTEE RESPONDED WITH A LETTER:

NO GIRLS (SHOULD BE) ALLOWED

"THERE ARE TENS OF THOUSANDS OF GIRLS WHO DEMAND THE RIGHT OF *COMPETITIONS*, AND THEY ARE GOING TO *GET* IT."

A COMPULSIVE SPORTS-WOMAN, BABE ALSO EXCELLED AT *TRACK AND FIELD*, WINNING TWO GOLD MEDALS AND ONE SILVER IN HURDLES, JAVELIN, AND HIGH JUMP, RESPECTIVELY, AT THE 1932 LOS ANGELES GAMES!

BABE DIDN'T CONFORM TO *ANYBODY'S* STEREOTYPES--CERTAINLY NOT AS A WOMAN, AND EVEN LESS SO AS A ROLE MODEL.

MANY OF HER GOLDEN CYCLONES TEAMMATES FOUND HER *SO ARROGANT* THAT THEY REFUSED TO ROOM WITH HER.

SHE LIKED TO *SPIT* OUT HOTEL WINDOWS TO SEE HOW MANY PEOPLE SHE COULD HIT ON THE HEAD ON THE SIDEWALK BELOW.

HAW! LOOK! I GOT THE FAT ONE!

SHE FURTHER ALIENATED HER TEAMMATES WHEN SHE DEMANDED MORE MONEY--EVEN AFTER McCOMBS RAISED HER SALARY TO $90.

BABE REFUSED TO *SHOOT* UNTIL SHE GOT A *RAISE*, AND GOT BENCHED.

THE PRESSURE TO SEND MONEY BACK HOME TO HER IMPOVERISHED PARENTS CLASHED WITH THE AAU'S STRICT ANTIPRO RULES.

BABE QUIT THE CYCLONES IN 1933 WHEN SHE WAS ACCUSED OF BEING PAID BY CHRYSLER TO PROMOTE A *CAR*--A NO-NO FOR AMATEUR ATHLETES.

NUTS TO *THIS!*

BABE DEFECTED TO PROFESSIONAL *GOLF* AND *TENNIS*, WHERE SHE WAS ALLOWED TO BECOME AS *RICH* AS HER SKILL AND FAME WOULD *ALLOW*.

PREDICTABLY, BY 1950 SHE HAD WON *EVERY* WOMEN'S GOLF TITLE THERE *WAS*.

HOOVER & CO. COULDN'T SHUT DOWN THE WOMEN'S *PROFESSIONAL* GAME, WHICH TOOK THE FORM OF ALL-FEMALE *BARNSTORMERS*.

ONE OF THE MORE FAMOUS AND LONG-LASTING WAS THE *ALL-AMERICAN RED HEADS* (1939-86) WHOSE PLAYERS WERE, OF COURSE, ALL *GINGERS*--NATURAL AND OTHERWISE.

THOUGH THEIR BEST PLAYER IN THE MID-1940S WAS SIX-TIME FREE-THROW CHAMPION *HAZEL WALKER*, A PART-*CHEROKEE* WHO REFUSED TO DYE HER BLACK HAIR, SO SHE WORE A *RED WIG* INSTEAD!

WALKER WOULD GO ON TO FOUND HER OWN BARNSTORMING TEAM, *HAZEL WALKER'S ARKANSAS TRAVELERS* (1949-65), MAKING HER THE FIRST FEMALE OWNER OF A PRO BASKETBALL TEAM!

AND TWO IMPORTANT SECTORS OF THE COUNTRY DEFIED HOOVER'S ANTIWOMEN'S SPORTS CRUSADE ENTIRELY.

AMERICA'S **BLACK SCHOOLS** SIMPLY **IGNORED** THE BAN ON GIRLS' TEAMS, LETTING THEIR FEMALE STUDENTS PASS, JUMP, AND SHOOT TO THEIR HEARTS' CONTENT.

(THE **BELLES** OF NORTH CAROLINA'S ALL-BLACK WOMEN'S **BENNETT COLLEGE** WENT UNDEFEATED IN 1934.)

ENTERTAINMENT-STARVED **RURAL AMERICA** ALSO REFUSED TO GIVE UP THEIR BELOVED WOMEN'S HOOPS ON THE SAY-SO OF **MONIED ELITES.**

IN **IOWA**, WOMEN'S COLLEGE BASKETBALL WAS MORE POPULAR THAN THE **MEN'S** GAME. THE STATE CHAMPIONSHIP IN DES MOINES WAS THE SPORTING EVENT OF THE YEAR.

A SCHOOL SUPERINTENDENT TOLD THE IOWA HIGH SCHOOL ASSOCIATION IN 1925 THAT ANYONE WHO WANTED TO BAN WOMEN'S SPORTS WOULD "BE STANDING IN THE CENTER OF THE TRACK WHEN **THE TRAIN RUNS OVER YOU.**"

OF COURSE, COLLEGE HOOPS WERE BIG IN THE **BIG CITIES** TOO.

THE **BIGGEST** COLLEGE TEAM IN AMERICA'S BIGGEST TOWN WAS THE BEAVERS OF THE **CITY COLLEGE OF NEW YORK** (CCNY).

C.C.N.Y.

ALLGAROO GAROO GARRA

C.C.N.Y.

AFTER LEAVING THE PROS, **ORIGINAL** ORIGINAL CELTIC **NAT HOLMAN** RETURNED TO HIS ALMA MATER TO COACH THE BEAVERS.

HEAR, HEAR, FELLOWS, **GOOD SHOW...**

HIS TEAMS BECAME THE **PRIDE** OF THE SCHOOL, AND THE PLAYERS LOVED THEIR WEIRDLY **ARISTOCRATIC** LEADER, THE EX-GHETTO KID WHO HAD STRIPPED ALL STREET AFFECT FROM HIS SPEECH.

THE *GOLD STANDARD* OF MEN'S COLLEGE BALL IN HOLMAN'S ERA WAS THE UNIVERSITY OF KENTUCKY *WILDCATS*.

KENTUCKY *DOMINATED* AFTER WORLD WAR II, WITH MANY EX-SERVICEMEN PLAYERS ATTENDING COLLEGE ON THE GI BILL.

THE DICTATORIAL COACH, *ADOLPH RUPP*, INSISTED ON CONDUCTING PRACTICES IN COMPLETE SILENCE.

IF THEY WANT TO *TALK*, WE'VE GOT A *STUDENT UNION* FOR *VISITING PURPOSES*.

WHEN THE WILDCATS MARCHED ONTO THE COURT, AN OPPONENT COMPARED THEM TO A *"ROMAN LEGION."*

KENTUCKY WON THE NCAA TOURNAMENT IN 1948 AND 1949 AND, HEADING INTO MADISON SQUARE GARDEN FOR THE 1950 NIT AGAINST CCNY, WERE WIDELY CONSIDERED THE BEST TEAM IN THE *WORLD*.

HOLMAN KNEW THAT RUPP HAD PUBLICLY DECLARED HE'D NEVER ALLOW A *BLACK PLAYER* ON HIS TEAM.

SO HE CANNILY SUGGESTED HIS THREE JEWISH AND TWO AFRICAN AMERICAN STARTERS TRY TO SHAKE THE WILDCATS' HANDS BEFORE THE GAME.

THE KENTUCKY PLAYERS TURNED THEIR *BACKS* ON THEM.

AS COACH HOLMAN SUSPECTED, THE SNUB *FIRED UP* HIS KIDS.

(DECADES LATER, EX-BEAVER FLOYD LAYNE WOULD TAKE OVER AS CCNY HEAD COACH.)

YOU'RE GONNA BE *PICKING COTTON* IN THE MORNING, MAN!

THE FINAL SCORE-- CCNY 81, KENTUCKY 50-- WAS THE *MOST BRUTAL LOSS* OF RUPP'S CAREER.

THE NIT CHAMPION BEAVERS WOULD GO ON TO WIN THE NCAA TOURNAMENT *TOO*, THEREBY SECURING THE FIRST--AND OF THIS WRITING, *ONLY*--"GRAND SLAM" IN COLLEGE HISTORY.

NEW YORK FANS LOVED THE COLLEGE GAME-- BUT NOT ALL FOR THE *SAME REASON*.

STUPID, WHAT ARE YOU DOING MAKING THAT BASKET?

YOU'RE FOUR OVER THE SPREAD!

WHEN NEWSPAPERS STARTED PRINTING THE FAVORED *POINT SPREADS* OF UPCOMING MATCHUPS, *GAMBLING* ON THEM BECAME THAT MUCH MORE ATTRACTIVE.

The World

CITY, JASPERS FAVORED OVER MISSOURI, SIENA

BETTING ON THE POINT SPREAD INSTEAD OF SIMPLY *WINNERS AND LOSERS* MADE THE GAMES THAT MUCH MORE EXCITING.

COLLEGE HOOPS SOON EARNED A REPUTATION AS *"THE SLOT MACHINE* OF SPORTS."

JACKPOT

IN THE SUMMER, MANY COLLEGE PLAYERS HEADED TO THE CATSKILL MOUNTAINS AS "WAITERS"--BUT THEIR *REAL* VOCATION WAS SINKING BUCKETS FOR THE SO-CALLED *"BORSCHT BELT LEAGUE."*

WHA-- SAY, AREN'T YOU *BOB COUSY?!*

SSHH!!

HOLY CROSS STAR *BOB COUSY* RETURNED HOME TO BROOKLYN FROM HIS SUMMER BORSCHT-BELT JOB ONE YEAR WITH *$1,400 IN SINGLES* IN A PAPER BAG. HIS FATHER HAD NEVER *SEEN* SO MUCH MONEY...

HELLO, OFFICERS?!

...AND HIS MOTHER NEARLY CALLED THE *COPS* ON HIM BECAUSE SHE THOUGHT HE HAD ROBBED A BANK!

BETTING ON THE BORSCHT-BELT LEAGUE WAS COMMONPLACE--AND *ENCOURAGED*. A HOTEL'S GUESTS WON A COLLECTIVE *POT* BASED ON TOTAL SCORES AT THE END OF THE SEASON.

HIGH-ROLLING MANHATTAN GAMBLER *SALVATORE "TATO" SOLLAZZO* BEGAN HANGING AROUND THE CATSKILLS RESORTS, CHATTING UP PLAYERS.

LOOK, NO ONE IS ASKING YOU TO *THROW* GAMES.

ALL MY FRIENDS AND I WANT...IS FOR YOU TO WIN BY *LESS*.

LOOK, YOU THINK YOUR *SCHOOL* AIN'T MAKING *BIG BUCKS* OFFA YOUR GAMES?

WISE UP! WHY SHOULDN'T *YOU* SEE SOME OF THAT SCRATCH?

CCNY'S PLAYERS WERE THE SONS OF *IMMIGRANTS* AND THE GRANDSONS OF *SLAVES*.

SOLLAZZO'S PITCH PROVED TOO *TEMPTING* TO RESIST.

THUNK

THE FIX IS CALLED *"POINT SHAVING"*--

--DOING WHAT YOU COULD TO KEEP THE SCORE *WITHIN* THE SPREAD DESIRED BY CROOKED GAMBLERS.

ONE ONLY NEEDED TO FLIP TWO OR THREE PLAYERS TO AFFECT THE OUTCOME OF AN ENTIRE GAME.

WHAT'S WRONG WITH YOU, AL? THAT WAS AN EASY LAYUP--GET YOUR HEAD IN THE GAME!

SORRY, COACH--GOT A BIG TEST TOMORROW...!

THE NCAA CONSIDERED POINT-SHAVING *CHEATING* AND THEREFORE *ILLEGAL.*

EDDIE GARD, A GUARD (NATURALLY) FOR LONG ISLAND UNIVERSITY (LIU), WAS SOLLAZZO'S *SUMMER CHAUFFEUR,* DRIVING FROM HOTEL TO HOTEL IN THE CATSKILLS TO MEET PLAYERS.

SOLLAZZO'S NAME BECAME KNOWN TO THE NYPD, AND SOON SO WAS GARD'S.

DETECTIVES TAILING GARD DISCOVERED HE WAS IN CONTACT WITH CCNY'S STAR PLAYERS. THEY'D MEET IN CENTRAL PARK TO PASS OFF SOLLAZZO'S PAYMENTS.

CCNY'S LOSSES BEGAN *MOUNTING,* CONSISTENTLY COMING IN *UNDER* THE SPREAD AGAINST FAR INFERIOR TEAMS--SHOOTING AT A BAFFLING 20 PERCENT.

FINALLY, A MANHATTAN COLLEGE STUDENT-PLAYER NAMED *JUNIUS KELLOGG* TOLD HIS COACH THAT AN EX-TEAMMATE HAD OFFERED HIM *$1,000* TO THROW AN UPCOMING GAME.

KELLOGG AND THE COACH WENT PUBLIC.

ANY ATHLETE IN THE COUNTRY, IN ANY COLLEGE, WOULD HAVE DONE THE SAME THING IF HE WAS FOR *CLEAN SPORTS* AND *CLEAN LIVING.*

WELL...NOT *ANY* ATHLETE, CLEARLY.

KELLOGG'S FLIP SPOOKED GARD AND SOLLAZZO, FORCING THE NYPD TO *ARREST* THE DUO BEFORE THEY COULD FLEE.

CCNY HAD BEEN PLAYING TEMPLE IN PHILADELPHIA. AS SOON AS THEIR TRAIN ENTERED THE UNDERWATER TUNNEL BETWEEN NEW JERSEY AND NEW YORK, THEREBY PASSING INTO THE NYPD'S *JURISDICTION*...

...THE DETECTIVES REVEALED THEMSELVES TO COACH HOLMAN.

WE'RE GONNA NEED TO BRING YOUR BOYS IN FOR QUESTIONING...

MY... *MY* BOYS?!

BUT CCNY WAS FAR FROM THE ONLY SCHOOL IMPLICATED.

TWO *KENTUCKY WILDCATS* CONFESSED TO POINT SHAVING FOR BRIBES DURING THEIR 1949 RUN.

THE NCAA DECLARED KENTUCKY *INELIGIBLE* FOR THE 1952-53 SEASON, AND WHEN THREE STAR PLAYERS HAD TO SIT OUT THE FOLLOWING YEAR DUE TO THEIR ROLE IN THE SCANDAL, THE WILDCATS HAD TO PASS ON THE 1954 TOURNEY.

COACH HOLMAN DENOUNCED THE BORSCHT BELT LEAGUE HOTELS AS *"SCHOOLS OF CRIME."*

OUT OF ORDER

THE SCANDAL FORCED CATSKILL RESORTS TO ELIMINATE BASKETBALL AS A SPECTATOR SPORT.

ALL OF THAT WAS *COLD COMFORT* TO HOLMAN.

THESE WERE HIS BOYS. HE HAD BEEN A GHETTO KID JUST LIKE THEM, LEARNING TO SHOOT FROM EVERY POSITION UNDER THE BASKETS OF SEWARD PARK UNTIL *THE WEE HOURS.*

HE HAD PUT HIS *FAITH* IN HIS BOYS, AND TRIED TO GUIDE THEM TO BECOME *BETTER MEN*.

AND CLEARLY, HE HAD *FAILED*.

HOLMAN WATCHED AS HIS PLAYERS WERE LED AWAY AND THEN HE TURNED AND DISAPPEARED DOWN THE PLATFORM.

ONE OF THE DETECTIVES SAID HOLMAN LOOKED LIKE HE HAD BEEN *"KICKED IN THE STOMACH."*

SEVEN CCNY PLAYERS-- INCLUDING 1950 HERO FLOYD LAYNE--WERE ACCUSED OF RECEIVING *$10,000* IN BRIBES TO SHAVE POINTS DURING VARIOUS GAMES.

BECAUSE THEY COOPERATED, ALL BUT *ONE* AVOIDED JAIL TIME. BUT MOST WERE DRUMMED OUT OF BASKETBALL FOREVER.

IT WAS BASKETBALL'S EQUIVALENT OF BASEBALL'S NEARLY-SPORT-ENDING *BLACK SOX SCANDAL*.

FORTUNATELY, FOR FANS WHO *LOST FAITH* IN THE COLLEGE GAME...

...*ANOTHER* FORM OF BASKETBALL WAS READY AND WILLING TO PICK UP THE SLACK!

Chapter Four
The Rise of the Pros

THE FALLOUT FROM THE POINT-SHAVING SCANDAL WAS *SO* BAD THAT MADISON SQUARE GARDEN CONSIDERED (BRIEFLY) *DROPPING* BASKETBALL ALTOGETHER.

HEY GUYS, WAIT UP, REMEMBER ME?!

OF COURSE, THERE WAS *ANOTHER* TEAM ASSOCIATED WITH MSG--THE *NEW YORK KNICKERBOCKERS,** ONE OF THE FOUNDING FRANCHISES OF THE *LATEST* ATTEMPT TO START A PRO B-BALL LEAGUE.

*"KNICKERBOCKER" IS AN OLD TERM FOR A (DUTCH) NEW YORKER, POPULARIZED BY *WASHINGTON "SLEEPY HOLLOW" IRVING*.

THE *BASKETBALL ASSOCIATION OF AMERICA* (BAA) STARTED IN 1946, LARGELY THE BRAINCHILD OF MSG'S DIRECTOR OF HOOPS, *NED IRISH*.

BASKETBALL ASSOCIATION OF AMERICA

IT IS OUR BELIEF THAT OUR EFFORTS TO INTRODUCE A *FOURTH* MAJOR SPORT WILL BE *STAMPED* WITH *SUCCESS*!

IT WASN'T GOING TO HAPPEN *OVERNIGHT*, THOUGH. THE KNICKS PLAYED MOST OF THEIR HOME GAMES IN THE *69TH REGIMENT ARMORY* TO AVOID THE EMBARRASSMENT OF A NEARLY *EMPTY* GARDEN.

(THE KNICKS' *ATTENDANCE* RECORD WAS A DISMAL *18,255* IN 1957...A YEAR IN WHICH BASEBALL'S NEW YORK YANKEES WOULD REGULARLY DRAW 70,000 *A GAME*.)

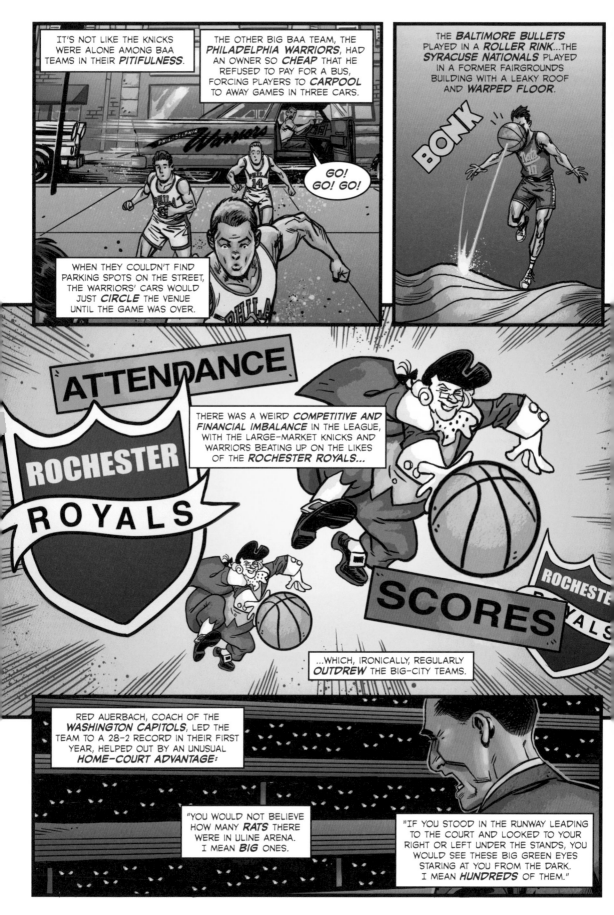

IT'S NOT LIKE THE KNICKS WERE ALONE AMONG BAA TEAMS IN THEIR *PITIFULNESS*.

THE OTHER BIG BAA TEAM, THE *PHILADELPHIA WARRIORS*, HAD AN OWNER SO *CHEAP* THAT HE REFUSED TO PAY FOR A BUS, FORCING PLAYERS TO *CARPOOL* TO AWAY GAMES IN THREE CARS.

GO! GO! GO!

WHEN THEY COULDN'T FIND PARKING SPOTS ON THE STREET, THE WARRIORS' CARS WOULD JUST *CIRCLE* THE VENUE UNTIL THE GAME WAS OVER.

THE *BALTIMORE BULLETS* PLAYED IN A *ROLLER RINK*...THE *SYRACUSE NATIONALS* PLAYED IN A FORMER FAIRGROUNDS BUILDING WITH A LEAKY ROOF AND *WARPED FLOOR*.

BONK

ATTENDANCE

ROCHESTER ROYALS

THERE WAS A WEIRD *COMPETITIVE AND FINANCIAL IMBALANCE* IN THE LEAGUE, WITH THE LARGE-MARKET KNICKS AND WARRIORS BEATING UP ON THE LIKES OF THE *ROCHESTER ROYALS*...

SCORES

ROCHESTER ROYALS

...WHICH, IRONICALLY, REGULARLY *OUTDREW* THE BIG-CITY TEAMS.

RED AUERBACH, COACH OF THE *WASHINGTON CAPITOLS*, LED THE TEAM TO A 28-2 RECORD IN THEIR FIRST YEAR, HELPED OUT BY AN UNUSUAL *HOME-COURT ADVANTAGE*:

"YOU WOULD NOT BELIEVE HOW MANY *RATS* THERE WERE IN ULINE ARENA. I MEAN *BIG* ONES.

"IF YOU STOOD IN THE RUNWAY LEADING TO THE COURT AND LOOKED TO YOUR RIGHT OR LEFT UNDER THE STANDS, YOU WOULD SEE THESE BIG GREEN EYES STARING AT YOU FROM THE DARK. I MEAN *HUNDREDS* OF THEM."

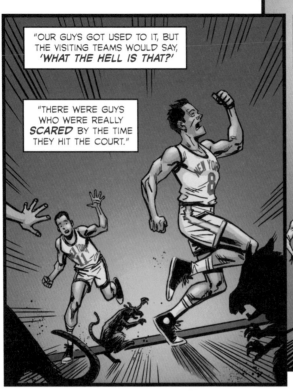

"OUR GUYS GOT USED TO IT, BUT THE VISITING TEAMS WOULD SAY, 'WHAT THE HELL IS THAT?'"

"THERE WERE GUYS WHO WERE REALLY SCARED BY THE TIME THEY HIT THE COURT."

FINALLY, THE CAPS WENT OUT AND BOUGHT "THE BIGGEST, MEANEST CAT WE COULD FIND.

"WE'D COME IN FOR A GAME AND THERE WOULD BE THE CAT ALL BEAT UP FROM FIGHTING WITH THE RATS.

"I MEAN, IT WAS CUT UP. HE GOT A LOT OF 'EM, BUT HE DIDN'T GET ALL OF THEM."

THE BAA'S PRIMARY COMPETITION WAS THE NATIONAL BASKETBALL LEAGUE (NBL), WHICH HAD BEEN AROUND SINCE 1935...

...ORIGINALLY NAMED THE MIDWEST BASKETBALL CONFERENCE (MBC), IT WAS COMPOSED PRIMARILY OF GREAT LAKES "INDUSTRIAL TEAMS" SPONSORED BY BIG CORPORATIONS, LIKE GENERAL ELECTRIC AND GOODYEAR.

THOUGH THE BAA BOASTED BIGGER MARKETS, THE NBL HAD BIGGER STARS, SHOWCASED BY THE CHICAGO AMERICAN GEARS' 6' 10" CENTER GEORGE MIKAN--ONE OF THE GAME'S FIRST "BIG MEN."

GEARS' OWNER MAURICE WHITE DEMANDED TO BE MADE PRESIDENT OF NBL, AND WHEN HE WAS REFUSED, FOUNDED HIS OWN LEAGUE, THE PROFESSIONAL BASKETBALL LEAGUE OF AMERICA. IT STRUGGLED ALONG UNTIL FOLDING THE FOLLOWING YEAR.

PBLA 1947-1948

WHITE'S PLAYERS WERE BROKEN UP AMONG THE OTHER PRO TEAMS, AND MIKAN FOUND HIMSELF ON THE BAA'S MINNEAPOLIS LAKERS.

AFTER FIGHTING OVER DRAFTEES AND NATIONAL COVERAGE FOR YEARS, THE TWO LEAGUES FINALLY DECIDED TO **COMBINE FORCES.**

ON AUGUST 3, 1949, THE BAA AND THE NBL MERGED INTO THE **NATIONAL BASKETBALL ASSOCIATION (NBA).**

(1969 NBA LOGO BASED ON A PHOTO OF LAKERS LEGEND **JERRY WEST**)

THE MERGER CAME AT AN **AUSPICIOUS** TIME, POSITIONING THE PROS TO TAKE ADVANTAGE OF SHAKEN PUBLIC FAITH IN THE COLLEGE GAME BECAUSE OF THE **POINT-SHAVING** SCANDAL...

...EVEN AS CURRENT NBA PLAYERS GOT **KICKED OUT** OF THE LEAGUE FOR TAKING BRIBES WHILE AT SCHOOL.

(CCNY DROPPED THE REST OF ITS 1951 SEASON BECAUSE OF THE SCANDAL.)

STILL, IT WAS A **STRUGGLE** TO PROVE THAT THE PROS COULD PROVIDE FANS WITH A **COMPARABLE** PRODUCT.

THE BOSTON CELTICS* HAD TO **PROVE** THEMSELVES TO BEANTOWN BY GOING TO WORCESTER AND **DEMOLISHING** HOLY CROSS.

"MOST NIGHTS, I'D TELL THE GUYS TO WIN BY THIRTY," REMEMBERED NEW COACH RED AUERBACH. "I WANTED TO BEAT HOLY CROSS BY **FIFTY.** PEOPLE **NOTICED.**"

* NO RELATION TO THE "ORIGINAL" (NEW YORK) CELTICS

CCNY

MOTH BALLS

A LOT OF WORCESTER FANS SHOWED UP TO WATCH THE RETURN OF A *HERO*.

IN BASKETBALL, *STYLE* IS AS IMPORTANT TO THE FAN AS THE SHEER *RESULT*.

THE SON OF FRENCH EMIGRANTS, *BOB COUSY* WAS A PLAY-MAKING SUBSTITUTE FOR HOLY CROSS DURING THEIR 1946–47 NCAA CHAMPIONSHIP YEAR.

AT A MERE 6' 1" AND 170 POUNDS, HE WAS, AS SOME SAID, *"NOT A PITUITARY FREAK"*--A NORMAL-SIZE PERSON THE FANS COULD RELATE TO.

(IMMORTALIZED IN A STATUE AT HIS ALMA MATER IN 2008)

ALL OF BOSTON WANTED THE CELTICS TO *DRAFT* COUSY WHEN HE GRADUATED. BUT AUERBACH, WHO WAS COACH *AND* GENERAL MANAGER, HAD DIFFERENT IDEAS.

AM I SUPPOSED TO *WIN*...OR PLEASE THE *LOCAL YOKELS*?

NEEDLESS TO SAY, FANS WERE *NOT* AMUSED.

RED DRAFTED A *"PITUITARY FREAK"* INSTEAD, AND COUSY WENT TO ANOTHER NBA TEAM, THE *CHICAGO STAGS*...

...BUT THE TEAM *COLLAPSED* BEFORE THE 1950–51 SEASON.

VIA THE *DISPERSAL DRAFT*, WHICH REDISTRIBUTED THE PLAYERS FROM FAILED TEAMS TO SURVIVORS, COUSY WOUND UP WITH BOSTON ANYWAY.

COUSY WILL HAVE TO *MAKE THE TEAM!*

HIS INCREDIBLE DRIBBLING AND PASSING SKILLS ENSURED THAT *"THE COOZ"* WAS NAMED TO THE ALL-NBA TEAM FOR *TEN STRAIGHT YEARS*, AND LED THE LEAGUE IN *ASSISTS* FOR EIGHT CONSECUTIVE SEASONS.

THE ONLY KICK I HAVE WITH COUSY IS THAT HE MAKES PRACTICE SESSIONS *HARD* ON A COACH.

ALL THE OTHER PLAYERS JUST WANT TO *STAND STILL* AND *WATCH* HIM!

NOW THOROUGHLY WON OVER, COACH AUERBACH BASED HIS ENTIRE *FAST-BREAK SYSTEM* AROUND HIS STAR.

NOT JUST AN OFFENSE, RED CALLED THE FAST BREAK A *"PHILOSOPHY"* AND A *"WAY OF LIFE."*

AS SOON AS AN OPPOSING TEAM MAKES A BASKET, THE OTHER TEAM GETS POSSESSION...

...TRANSFORMING DEFENSIVE PLAYERS INTO OFFENSIVE PLAYERS.

RED ALWAYS WANTED HIS TEAMS TO GET THE BALL TO THE OTHER END OF THE COURT AS QUICKLY AS POSSIBLE...

...TAKING ADVANTAGE OF COUSY'S ABILITY TO MAKE THE LONG PASS!

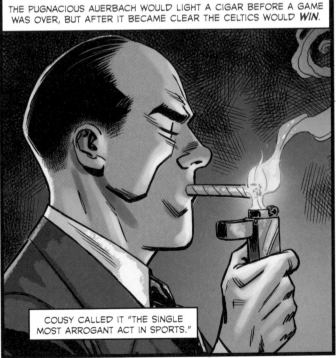

THE PUGNACIOUS AUERBACH WOULD LIGHT A CIGAR BEFORE A GAME WAS OVER, BUT AFTER IT BECAME CLEAR THE CELTICS WOULD *WIN.*

COUSY CALLED IT "THE SINGLE MOST ARROGANT ACT IN SPORTS."

RED SWORE, "I NEVER DID IT ON THE ROAD-- *NEVER*. THAT WOULD HAVE BEEN *RUBBING IT IN*.

"OF COURSE, ONE NIGHT WE WENT INTO CINCINNATI, AND I FOUND OUT THEY'D GIVEN OUT *FIVE THOUSAND CIGARS* AND TOLD THE FANS WHEN THE ROYALS WON THE GAME THEY SHOULD ALL LIGHT UP.

"I SAID TO THE GUYS IN THE LOCKER ROOM BEFORE THE GAME:

"IF YOU DON'T *WIN* THIS ONE, I'LL *KILL* YOU!"

CELTICS 17

(THE CELTICS WON.)

THE CELTICS' MAIN RIVALS, THE MINNEAPOLIS LAKERS, WON *FIVE* OF THE FIRST *SIX* NBA CROWNS.

MADISON SQ GARDEN

TONITE: GEORGE MIKAN VS THE NEW YORK KNICKS

"MR. BASKETBALL," GEORGE MIKAN, WAS SO POPULAR, HE OVERSHADOWED HIS OWN TEAM.

THE LAKERS WERE *BALL CONTROL SPECIALISTS*, STALLING THE CLOCK TO GET THEIR GIANT BENEATH THE BASKET FOR AN EASY SHOT.

"WAITING FOR MIKAN," FRUSTRATED PLAYERS CALLED IT, IN REFERENCE TO THE DISMAL BECKETT PLAY *WAITING FOR GODOT*.

THANKS TO THEIR RESPECTIVE STARS, THE CELTICS AND THE MINNEAPOLIS LAKERS *DOMINATED* THE EARLY NBA.

THROUGH 2010, IN FACT, THE CELTICS AND LAKERS WON *THIRTY-THREE TITLES*-- THAT'S *HALF* OF ALL NBA CHAMPIONSHIPS, PERIOD!

IN A NOVEMBER 23, 1950, GAME, THE FORT WAYNE PISTONS GAVE MINNEAPOLIS A TASTE OF ITS OWN MEDICINE, ENDING THE LAKERS' TWENTY-NINE-GAME HOME WINNING STREAK BY TAKING *KEEP AWAY* TO NEW HEIGHTS, FREEZING THE BALL LONG ENOUGH TO STEAL A 19-18 VICTORY.

THOUGH IT WAS A WINNING STRATEGY, WATCHING GUYS PASS TO EACH OTHER ALL GAME WAS ALSO EXCEEDINGLY *DULL TO WATCH.*

EPITOMIZING THE NBA'S *MOLASSES* RATE OF PLAY WAS A MARCH 20, 1954, PLAYOFF BETWEEN THE KNICKS AND CELTICS THAT LASTED *THREE HOURS.*

UP NEXT: RERUNS OF TEST PATTERNS

THE GAME WAS *SO BORING* THAT THE TV STATION CARRYING IT SIMPLY *CUT AWAY* IN THE FINAL SECONDS.

SYRACUSE NATIONALS' OWNER *DANNY BIASONE* WAS FED UP WITH THE PROS' SLUGGISHNESS.

SOMETHING HAS TO BE DONE!

UP NEXT: RERUNS OF TEST PATTERNS

"I LOOKED AT THE *BOX SCORES* FROM THE GAMES I *ENJOYED*, GAMES WHERE THEY DIDN'T SCREW AROUND AND *STALL.*

GAMES THAT DIDN'T STINK:
NATIONA
CELTICS
KNICKS V
NATIONA
ROYALS
CELTICS
WARRIOR
NATIONAL
NATIONAL

MAKE NBA NOT BORING: HOW?
-GIVE PLAYERS JETPACKS?
-SET BALL ON FIRE?
-SPIDERS?

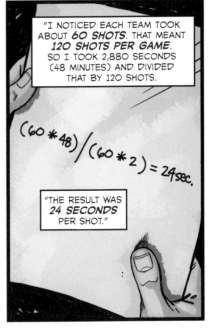

"I NOTICED EACH TEAM TOOK ABOUT *60 SHOTS*. THAT MEANT *120 SHOTS PER GAME.* SO I TOOK 2,880 SECONDS (48 MINUTES) AND DIVIDED THAT BY 120 SHOTS.

$$(60 * 48) / (60 * 2) = 24 sec.$$

"THE RESULT WAS *24 SECONDS* PER SHOT."

BIASONE AND HIS GENERAL MANAGER, *LEO FARRIS*, CONVINCED THE NBA TO ADOPT THE SHOT CLOCK FOR THE 1954–55 SEASON.

THE OFFENSE HAD *24 SECONDS* AFTER TAKING POSSESSION TO TAKE A SHOT OR RISK A TURNOVER.

(SYRACUSE'S ARMORY SQUARE INSTALLED A MONUMENT TO THE SHOT CLOCK IN 2005.)

THE BALL HAD TO BE *IN THE AIR* BEFORE TIME WAS UP FOR THE SHOT TO COUNT.

HOOOONK

THE EFFECTS ON THE GAME WERE *INSTANTANEOUS*. AVERAGE SCORING ROSE FROM 79.5 TO *93.1* POINTS PER GAME, AND BIASONE'S NATIONALS WERE REWARDED WITH THE NBA CHAMPIONSHIP THAT YEAR.

MVP

THE CELTICS' *RED AUERBACH* WAS THE FIRST COACH TO FULLY *EXPLOIT* THE NEW SHOT-CLOCK ERA, WHICH COMPLEMENTED HIS ALREADY RAPID-FIRE *FAST-BREAK* OFFENSE.

HE'D MANIPULATE THE CLOCK IN OTHER WAYS TOO.

ORIGINALLY, TEAMS WOULD PLAY THEIR FIVE BEST PLAYERS AND SAT THEM OUT ONLY WHEN THEY TIRED. RED DID THE *OPPOSITE*.

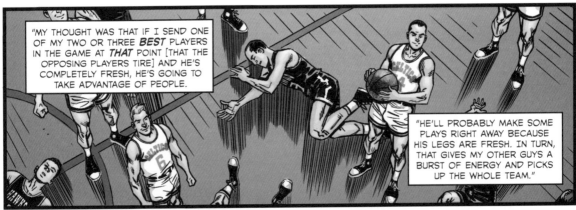

"MY THOUGHT WAS THAT IF I SEND ONE OF MY TWO OR THREE *BEST* PLAYERS IN THE GAME AT *THAT* POINT [THAT THE OPPOSING PLAYERS TIRE] AND HE'S COMPLETELY FRESH, HE'S GOING TO TAKE ADVANTAGE OF PEOPLE.

"HE'LL PROBABLY MAKE SOME PLAYS RIGHT AWAY BECAUSE HIS LEGS ARE FRESH. IN TURN, THAT GIVES MY OTHER GUYS A BURST OF ENERGY AND PICKS UP THE WHOLE TEAM."

MANY STARS ACCUSTOMED TO THE OLD STYLE OF PLAY FLED THE SHOT-CLOCK ERA ENTIRELY.

I WILL PROVE MY CLIENT'S INNOCENCE WITH A SERIES OF *EASY LAYUPS...*

PERHAPS SENSING THE WAY THE WINDS OF THE GAME WERE BLOWING, AFTER THE LAKERS WON THE TITLE IN 1954, *GEORGE MIKAN* RETIRED AT THE RIPE OLD AGE OF *TWENTY-NINE* TO BECOME A LAWYER.

EVEN *WITHOUT* MIKAN, THE LAKERS WON THE 1956 NBA CHAMPIONSHIP.

THEY WOULD BE THE LAST *ALL-WHITE* TEAM TO WIN THE TITLE.

THOUGH MANY OF THE BIG *COLLEGE* TEAMS WERE FROM *INTEGRATED SCHOOLS*, WHERE BLACKS AND WHITES PLAYED TOGETHER ALL THE TIME, THE NBA REFRAINED FROM DRAFTING *BLACK PLAYERS* BECAUSE OF ONE MAN...

...*ABE SAPERSTEIN*, WHO WANTED THE BEST AFRICAN AMERICAN STARS FOR HIS HARLEM GLOBETROTTERS, WHICH *STILL* OUTDREW *ALL NBA TEAMS*.

MINE!

ALSO, SOME OWNERS AND EXECUTIVES WORRIED THAT A PREPONDERANCE OF *BLACK PLAYERS* WOULD DRIVE *WHITE FANS* FROM THE GAME.

RED AUERBACH HAD ALREADY INFURIATED SAPERSTEIN BY DRAFTING THE NBA'S FIRST AFRICAN AMERICAN PLAYER, **CHUCK COOPER**, IN 1950.

ABE THREATENED TO HAVE THE GLOBETROTTERS **BOYCOTT** BOSTON GARDEN-- NO IDLE THREAT.

BUT RED NEEDED A **CENTER** SKILLED AT **SHOT BLOCKING** AND **REBOUNDING** TO COMPLEMENT BOB COUSY'S PASSING AND SCORING SKILLS.

SO HE IGNORED SAPERSTEIN'S COMPLAINTS AND DRAFTED **BILL RUSSELL**, A STAR WITH THE NCAA CHAMPION DONS OF THE UNIVERSITY OF SAN FRANCISCO.

BAKE SALE

THE HUMBLE DONS HAD NO GYM AND WERE FORCED TO PRACTICE AT A NEARBY **HIGH SCHOOL**.

NEVERTHELESS THE 1955-56 TEAM BECAME THE FIRST TEAM TO GO **UNDEFEATED** SINCE THE FOUNDING OF THE NCAA, WINNING BY AN AVERAGE OF **20 POINTS**!

THE CELTICS WERE ABLE TO **STEAL** RUSSELL FROM FIRST-PICKING ROCHESTER WHEN CELTICS' OWNER WALTER BROWN OFFERED THE ROYALS' OWNER THE **ICE CAPADES** IN EXCHANGE FOR GIVING UP THE USF STAR.

RUSSELL WAS AN INTENSE PLAYER WHO **THREW UP** BEFORE EVERY GAME. (HIS TEAMMATES SOON STARTED TO GREET THE SOUNDS OF VOMITING AS A POSITIVE SIGN.)

HHRRRGGHHH!!

YEAH!! A "W" TONIGHT!

RUSSELL BROUGHT THAT INTENSITY **ONTO THE COURT** AND DIRECTED IT AT HIS OPPONENTS. HE IS THE MOST FEARED DEFENDER IN THE GAME'S HISTORY.

"THERE WASN'T A GUY I JUMPED AGAINST I COULDN'T **BEAT** IF I HAD THE CHANCE TO TALK TO HIM BEFOREHAND," HE SAID.

THREE TONIGHT.

GUESS **WHICH** THREE.

GULP!

HALL-OF-FAMER ELVIN HAYES CALLED RUSSELL *"THE GHOST"* BECAUSE YOU NEVER SAW HIM BEFORE HE SUDDENLY *MATERIALIZED* TO BLOCK YOUR SHOT.

THAT'S *ONE.*

AS RUSSELL FAMOUSLY SAID, "THE IDEA IS NOT TO BLOCK *EVERY* SHOT. THE IDEA IS TO MAKE YOUR OPPONENT BELIEVE THAT YOU *MIGHT* BLOCK EVERY SHOT."

THAT'S *TWO.*

AN OPPOSING GM ONCE SAID, "SURE, *RED AUERBACH* MAKES MISTAKES, THE ENTIRE BOSTON *TEAM* MAKES MISTAKES.

"BUT THEY CAN *GET AWAY WITH IT* BECAUSE THEY HAVE THE WORLD'S LARGEST *ERASER* IN BILL RUSSELL."

AND THERE'S *THREE!*

THE CELTICS WON THEIR FIRST NBA TITLE IN 1957. LED BY RED AND RUSSELL, BOSTON WOULD WIN *ELEVEN* CHAMPIONSHIPS THROUGH 1969 AS *THE* DOMINANT PRO TEAM OF THIS PERIOD.

THE FEARED *"WHITE FLIGHT"* OF CAUCASIAN FANS NEVER MATERIALIZED.

THOUGH COLLEGE HOOPS REMAINED (AND *REMAINS*) SUPER-POPULAR, THE POINT-SHAVING SCANDAL *PLUS* THE SHOT CLOCK *PLUS* RACIAL INTEGRATION...

...MEANT THAT NED IRISH'S DREAM OF A *FOURTH* MAJOR PRO SPORT IN AMERICA WAS FINALLY REALIZED!

CHAPTER FIVE
LEAGUE WARS

FACING A SUDDENLY ROBUST PRO LEAGUE, ABE SAPERSTEIN SOON DISCOVERED HIS FEARS ABOUT THE ADDED COMPETITION FOR PLAYERS WERE NOT ENTIRELY *UNFOUNDED*.

SOME OF HIS GLOBETROTTERS *DEFECTED* TO THE NBA BECAUSE NOW THEY COULD.

THE MOST SUCCESSFUL DEFECTOR WAS UNDOUBTEDLY *WILT CHAMBERLAIN*.

A GIANT AMONG GIANTS AT 7' 1", *WILT THE STILT* WAS *SO* EFFECTIVE AT THE COLLEGE LEVEL THAT BY THE TIME HE LEFT SCHOOL, THE NCAA HAD *OUTLAWED* THREE OF HIS PERSONAL SPECIALTIES:

TAKING OFF FROM THE FOUL LINE AND *DUNKING* FREE THROWS;

OFFENSIVE GOALTENDING;

AND LOBBING INBOUND PASSES FROM THE BASELINE *OVER* THE BACKBOARD TO SINK THEM.

BORED WITH THE LEVEL OF COMPETITION IN THE NCAA, WILT DROPPED OUT OF THE UNIVERSITY OF KANSAS *BEFORE* HE WAS ELIGIBLE FOR THE NBA; WHILE WAITING, HE JOINED THE GLOBETROTTERS FOR THE 1958-59 SEASON.

THE TROTTERS TOURED THE SOVIET UNION THAT YEAR AND WERE GREETED BY *NIKITA KHRUSHCHEV*.

WILT JOINED THE NBA'S *PHILADELPHIA WARRIORS* AND BECAME THE ARCH-NEMESIS OF THE CELTICS' BILL RUSSELL.

IN HIS *FIRST* SEASON, HE BROKE THE ALL-TIME REGULAR-SEASON SCORING RECORD SET BY HAWKS LEGEND *BOB PETTIT*.

THE STILT REMAINS THE *ONLY* PLAYER TO SCORE 100 POINTS IN A *SINGLE GAME* AND AVERAGE MORE THAN 40 AND 50 POINTS A SEASON.

HIS ONLY WEAKNESS SEEMED TO BE HIS PITIFUL *FREE THROW RECORD*, WHICH WOULD PLAGUE HIM HIS WHOLE CAREER (.511).

ONE OF THE FEW PLACES WHERE HIS SUPERHUMAN PHYSICAL GIFTS WERE LARGELY INEFFECTUAL WAS AT THE LINE.

FEW WERE AS IMPRESSED BY WILT *AS* WILT.

WHAT SIGN WERE YOU BORN UNDER?

"THE *DOLLAR* SIGN!"

BUT BECAUSE RUSSELL'S CELTICS HAD THE *ELEVEN* CHAMPIONSHIPS TO WILT'S TWO (WITH THE NOW-*SAN FRANCISCO* WARRIORS AND NOW-*LOS ANGELES* LAKERS), CHAMBERLAIN LABORED UNDER THE GREAT DEFENDER'S SHADOW.

HARLEM HIGH SCHOOL PLAYER *LEW ALCINDOR* WAS A STUDENT OF BOTH WILT CHAMBERLAIN *AND* BILL RUSSELL, AND TRIED TO SEE THEM BOTH PLAY AS OFTEN AS HE COULD AT MADISON SQUARE GARDEN.

THAT COULD BE *YOU* SOME DAY, LEW!

YEAH, RIGHT...

"BUT SECRETLY," HE'D WRITE LATER, "I DIDN'T THINK I *COULD* BE LIKE THEM, I KNEW I *WOULD* BE LIKE THEM. MAYBE *BETTER*."

LEW WAS A *LARGE* YOUNG MAN, 6' 8" BY THE *EIGHTH GRADE* AND ALREADY ABLE TO *SLAM DUNK* ON A REGULATION HOOP.

WHEN YOU ARE THE *TALLEST* KID ON YOUR BLOCK, ON *ANY* BLOCK IN YOUR NEIGHBORHOOD, YOU *PLAY BASKETBALL!*

HE WAS A LEGENDARY HIGH SCHOOL BALLER FOR POWER MEMORIAL HIGH SCHOOL, KNOWN AS THE *"TOWER FROM POWER."*

LEW WAS A *SHY*, QUIET GIANT-- UNTIL HE STEPPED ON THE COURT.

HE GOT CAUGHT UP IN A RIOT IN HARLEM IN THE SUMMER OF 1964, AND IT FRIGHTENED HIM BADLY.

(FOR ONE THING, AT HIS SIZE HE WAS AN *EASY TARGET*.)

SO HE LITERALLY WENT ACROSS THE CONTINENT TO THE UNIVERSITY OF CALIFORNIA, LOS ANGELES (UCLA), ALMA MATER OF *JACKIE ROBINSON* AND *RAFER JOHNSON*, A BLACK OLYMPIC DECATHLON GOLD MEDALIST WHO HAD BEEN STUDENT BODY *PRESIDENT*.

THEY LET BLACK ATHLETES *THRIVE* HERE!

LEW HAD ALSO HEARD *GLOWING PRAISE* HEAPED ON THE HEAD OF UCLA'S PROGRAM, COACH *JOHN WOODEN.*

FOR MOST STUDENTS, BASKETBALL IS *TEMPORARY.* BUT *KNOWLEDGE* IS FOREVER.

LEW WAS IMPRESSED AT HOW LITTLE THEY TALKED ABOUT *SPORTS* IN THEIR INITIAL MEETING--WOODEN PREFERRED TO DISCUSS LEW'S ACADEMIC AMBITIONS AND PLANS FOR *LIFE.*

I'M SURE WE WILL FIND THE PROPER WAY TO USE YOU ON THE COURT.

I AM *LOOKING FORWARD* TO COACHING SOMEONE LIKE YOU.

AFTER HIS HARDSCRABBLE INDIANA UPBRINGING, *"JOHN-BOB"* SERVED IN THE NAVY DURING WWII AND HAD ALREADY HAD A DISTINGUISHED COACHING CAREER AT THE HIGH SCHOOL AND COLLEGE LEVEL BEFORE JOINING UCLA FOR THE 1948-49 SEASON.

GOOD MORNING, GENTLEMEN.

GOOD MORNING, COACH.

TODAY WE ARE GOING TO LEARN HOW TO PUT ON OUR SNEAKERS AND SOCKS *CORRECTLY.*

)SNORT!(

TUG. AND. *SNUG.*

IF YOU DO NOT PULL YOUR SOCKS ON *TIGHTLY,* YOU'RE LIKELY TO GET *WRINKLES* IN THEM.

WRINKLES CAUSE *BLISTERS.* BLISTERS FORCE PLAYERS TO SIT ON THE *SIDELINE.*

AND PLAYERS SITTING ON THE SIDELINE *LOSE GAMES.* SO WE ARE NOT JUST GOING TO *TUG.* WE ARE GOING TO ALSO MAKE *SNUG.*

LEW WOULD REMEMBER LOOKING UP TO THE RAFTERS OF PAULEY PAVILION DURING PRACTICE AND SEE WOODEN UP THERE, WATCHING THEM.

"HE WOULD LOOK DOWN AT US LIKE A *BENEVOLENT GOD*, WATCHING US SCUTTLE UP AND DOWN THE COURT."

DON'T THINK ABOUT *WINNING* THE GAME.

JUST DO EVERYTHING POSSIBLE TO *PREPARE.*

AS LONG AS YOU KNOW YOU HAVE DONE *EVERYTHING POSSIBLE* AND YOU HAVE GIVEN YOUR *BEST SELF* ON THE COURT, *THAT* IS YOUR REWARD.

THE SCOREBOARD IS MEANINGLESS.

LEW WOULD LATER WRITE, "TRYING TO APPLY (WOODEN'S) PHILOSOPHY SOLELY TOWARD *WINNING* WOULD BE LIKE DOING *GOOD DEEDS* ONLY BECAUSE YOU HOPE IT WILL GET YOU INTO *HEAVEN.*

"BEING GOOD *IS* THE PAYOFF, ATHLETICALLY AND SPIRITUALLY."

BEFORE WOODEN RETIRED IN 1975, THE "WIZARD OF WESTWOOD" WOULD BRING *TEN* NATIONAL CHAMPIONSHIPS TO UCLA, INCLUDING *SEVEN IN A ROW-- FOUR* OF THOSE WITH LEW ALCINDOR ON HIS SQUAD.

LEW WAS **SO** EFFECTIVE OFFENSIVELY THAT THE NCAA GAVE HIM THE WILT CHAMBERLAIN TREATMENT--BUT WHILE HE WAS STILL **IN** SCHOOL! THE **DUNK SHOT** WAS DECLARED "NOT SKILLFUL" AND **BANNED** BEFORE HIS JUNIOR YEAR.

FEW WERE FOOLED. THE BAN QUICKLY BECAME KNOWN AS *"THE LEW ALCINDOR RULE."*

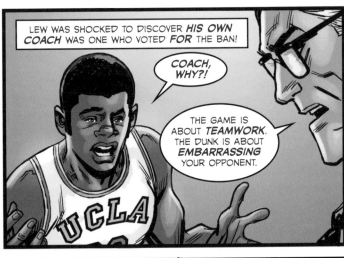

LEW WAS SHOCKED TO DISCOVER **HIS OWN COACH** WAS ONE WHO VOTED **FOR** THE BAN!

COACH, WHY?!

THE GAME IS ABOUT **TEAMWORK**. THE DUNK IS ABOUT **EMBARRASSING** YOUR OPPONENT.

LEW PROBABLY WOULD HAVE BEEN MORE UPSET HAD WOODEN NOT HELPED HIM DEVELOP ITS **REPLACEMENT**.

HIS COACH CALLED IT "LEWIS'S **FLAT HOOK**."

FAILING TO **PREPARE** IS PREPARING TO **FAIL**!

WOODEN WORKED WITH ALCINDOR ON A **SKYHOOK SHOT** INSPIRED BY GEORGE MIKAN.

"AS COACH INSTRUCTED, I'D REACH OUT WITH MY LEFT FOREARM TO CREATE DISTANCE FROM THE DEFENDER IN FRONT OF ME...PIVOT...

"...AND LAUNCH MYSELF INTO THE AIR FROM MY LEFT FOOT, RELEASING THE BALL SOFTLY FROM MY RIGHT HAND AND SHOOTING DOWN AT THE BASKET.

"HE WAS **RIGHT**: IT WAS VIRTUALLY IMPOSSIBLE FOR ANYONE TO EITHER **PREVENT** ME FROM GETTING IT OFF OR **BLOCKING** IT."

AS LEW NEARED GRADUATION, PRO TEAMS BEGAN TO CIRCLE, *DESPERATE* TO SIGN HIM.

THE MOST *ENTHUSIASTIC* TO RETAIN ALCINDOR'S SERVICES WAS THE NBA'S PRIMARY COMPETITION SINCE 1967, THE *AMERICAN BASKETBALL ASSOCIATION (ABA)*.

THE ABA WAS THE BRAINCHILD OF THE MAYOR OF BUENA PARK, CALIFORNIA, *DENNIS MURPHY*.

MURPHY HAD KIND OF A *THING* FOR SECOND SPORTS LEAGUES, GOING ON TO FOUND THE WORLD *HOCKEY* ASSOCIATION AND WORLD TEAM *TENNIS*.

IT WAS VISIONARY-- OR *DELUSIONAL*-- TO THINK A *SECOND* PRO B-BALL LEAGUE WOULD WORK.

BEAT IT, SMALL FRY!

THE NBA'S *CELTICS* WON THE CHAMPIONSHIP EVERY YEAR, BUT WERE STILL OUTDRAWN EVERY YEAR BY THE NHL'S BOSTON BRUINS... *IN THEIR OWN BUILDING*.

"WE HAD *NO PLAN*," SAID LEGAL COUNSEL TO THE INDIANA PACERS, ONE OF THE BIGGEST ABA FRANCHISES. "*NONE*."

ABA PLAN:
1. Form League
2. ?????
3. PROFIT

"WE WANTED TO START A SECOND LEAGUE AND FORCE THE NBA TO *MERGE* WITH US. *THAT* WAS THE GOAL."

THE ABA'S ORGANIZERS SHREWDLY BROUGHT IN *"MR. BASKETBALL"* HIMSELF TO BE THE FACE OF THE LEAGUE--*GEORGE MIKAN*, RETIRED SUPERSTAR.

MIKAN AGREED TO THEIR KOOKY PLAN, BUT HE HAD *THREE* STIPULATIONS.

FIRST, MIKAN OWNED A TRAVEL AGENCY AND PRACTICED LAW IN *MINNEAPOLIS*. HE DIDN'T WANT TO *MOVE*, SO HE INSISTED THAT ABA HEADQUARTERS HAD TO BE THERE TOO.

SECOND, MIKAN DEMANDED A *COLORFUL BALL* BECAUSE HIS EYESIGHT WAS BAD AND HE HAD TROUBLE FOLLOWING THE *BROWN* BALL IN REGULAR NBA GAMES.

COULD BE A BALL...COULD BE A *BEE*...!

THE TRICOLOR BALL DEFINED THE ABA'S BRASH, IN-YOUR-FACE STYLE.

KIDS *LOVED* IT, AND IT BECAME A POPULAR GIVEAWAY.

ONE OF THE FIRST TEAMS WAS IN *DENVER*, BUT THEY DIDN'T YET HAVE A TRICOLOR BALL FOR AN EXHIBITION GAME.

SO THEY SPRAY-PAINTED A REGULAR BALL RED, WHITE, AND BLUE.

IT MADE THE BALL SO SLIPPERY THERE WERE FORTY-FOUR TURNOVERS--*IN THE FIRST HALF!*

GENE LITTLES, MEMBER OF THE ABA'S CAROLINA COUGARS (1969-74) AND ABA CHAMPIONS KENTUCKY COLONELS (1974-75), SAID:

"IT WAS A SPECIAL FEELING TO TAKE A LONG SHOT AND WATCH THOSE COLORS *ROTATE* IN THE AIR... IT MADE YOUR HEART BEAT JUST A LITTLE *FASTER* WHEN YOU HIT A 25-FOOTER WITH THE ABA BALL."

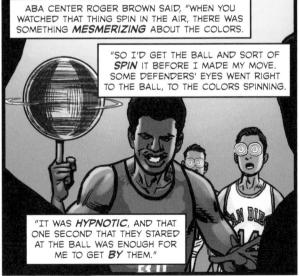

ABA CENTER ROGER BROWN SAID, "WHEN YOU WATCHED THAT THING SPIN IN THE AIR, THERE WAS SOMETHING *MESMERIZING* ABOUT THE COLORS.

"SO I'D GET THE BALL AND SORT OF *SPIN* IT BEFORE I MADE MY MOVE. SOME DEFENDERS' EYES WENT RIGHT TO THE BALL, TO THE COLORS SPINNING.

"IT WAS *HYPNOTIC*, AND THAT ONE SECOND THAT THEY STARED AT THE BALL WAS ENOUGH FOR ME TO GET *BY* THEM."

AND MIKAN'S **THIRD** DEMAND PROVED EVEN **MORE** CONSEQUENTIAL:

LET'S ESTABLISH A **THREE-POINT** "FIELD GOAL" LINE 25 FEET FROM THE BASKET!

THE COMMISH

"WE CALLED IT THE **HOME RUN**," MIKAN SAID, "BECAUSE THE 3-POINTER WAS EXACTLY THAT. IT BROUGHT THE FANS OUT OF THEIR SEATS."

HALL OF FAME COACH HUBIE BROWN RECALLED THAT WITH THE 3-POINTER "YOU HAVE TO TELL YOUR PLAYERS TO REMEMBER WHO THE **SHOOTERS** ARE...

"...AND WHEN THOSE GUYS ARE 25 FEET FROM THE BASKET, **GET IN THEIR JOCKS** AND GUARD THEM."

IT WAS BRASH, COLORFUL, AND **BOLD**--BUT THE ABA STRUGGLED TO WREST EYEBALLS AWAY FROM THE NBA, AND THE PLAYERS DEVELOPED **UNDERDOG CHIPS** ON THEIR SHOULDERS. GENE LITTLES REMEMBERS:

WE HAD THIS IMMENSE PRIDE THAT, RIGHT OR NOT, WE WERE **AS GOOD** IF NOT **BETTER** THAN THE NBA.

THE DIFFERENCE WAS THAT **THEY** HAD TELEVISION AND WE **DIDN'T**.

colonels 22

V

THE NETWORKS SHOWED NBA GAMES ONLY ON **SUNDAY AFTERNOONS**, AND THEN ONLY THOSE THAT FEATURED SUPERSTARS BILL RUSSELL OR WILT CHAMBERLAIN--OR, IDEALLY, **BOTH**.

STILL, TV TREATED BASKETBALL AS **THIRD FIDDLE** TO BASEBALL AND FOOTBALL.

ABA OWNERS OUTDID THE NBA IN VARIOUS SCHEMES TO ATTRACT THE ATTENTION OF AMERICA'S EYEBALLS.

HEY, WHEN DOES THE GAME START?

THERE'S A *GAME*?!

THE PACERS HAD A *WRESTLING BEAR*. THE DENVER ROCKETS HAD *"HALTER TOP" NIGHT.* IN MIAMI, THE FLORIDIANS' *"BALL GIRLS"* WERE MORE POPULAR THAN THE TEAM ITSELF.

THE *KENTUCKY COLONELS* SIGNED A *JOCKEY* NAMED *PENNY ANN EARLY* AS THE *FIRST FEMALE PLAYER* TO A PRO BASKETBALL CONTRACT.

THE COACH WAS *NOT* ON BOARD, THOUGH, AND HE PLAYED HER EXACTLY *ONE MINUTE* IN *ONE GAME*.

ALL SHE DID WAS THROW *AN INBOUNDS PASS*--BUT IT GOT HER IN THE *RECORD BOOKS!*

FWEEEEE!!

THE COLONELS ALSO HAD A TEN-WOMAN BOARD OF DIRECTORS IN CHARGE OF THE TEAM FOR THE 1972-73 SEASON, SO *GENDER DIVERSITY* WAS A *BIG DEAL* WITH THEM.

YOU'RE ABSOLUTELY RIGHT IN SAYING THAT I KNOW NOTHING ABOUT *BASKETBALL*...

...BUT MY HUSBAND KNOWS NOTHING ABOUT *MAKING CHICKEN* AND HE'S DONE *ALL RIGHT.*

THE OWNER OF *KENTUCKY FRIED CHICKEN*, JOHN Y. BROWN JR., HAD BOUGHT THE TEAM AND MADE HIS WIFE, *ELLIE*, THE CHAIRWOMAN.

WHEN THE COLONELS WON THE 1975 ABA CHAMPIONSHIP, THEY THREW ELLIE BROWN IN THE *SHOWER*, AS WAS *TRADITIONAL*.

COMPETITION BETWEEN THE NBA AND ABA TO SIGN TALENT WAS *BRUTAL*.

RATHER THAN *TEAMS* SIGNING PLAYERS, THE ABA WOULD *COLLECTIVELY POOL* ITS MONEY TO RAISE OFFERS.

PACERS EXEC DICK TINKHAM REMEMBERS THAT "OUR STANDARD LINE WAS THAT A MERGER WITH THE NBA IS *COMING* AND WHEN IT DOES, YOU'LL GO INTO A *COMMON DRAFT* AND YOU'LL HAVE TO SIGN WITH THE TEAM THAT PICKS YOU."

IT WAS RUMORED THAT THE ABA *BRIBED AGENTS* TO STEER THEIR CLIENTS *AWAY* FROM THE NBA.

THE ABA ALSO ACCEPTED PLAYERS *BANNED* FROM THE NBA FOR *POINT SHAVING*.

THE RIVALRY GOT *SO* INTENSE THAT ABA OWNERS DISCOVERED THE NBA *BUGGED* THEIR ANNUAL MEETING IN DENVER!

(OF COURSE, THE ABA HAD SPIES IN THE NBA TOO.)

THE ABA WAS PARTICULARLY DESPERATE TO RETAIN UCLA STAR *LEW ALCINDOR'S* SERVICES, AS HE WOULD GIVE THE UPSTART LEAGUE INSTANT LEGITIMACY.

THEY CALLED THEIR SECRET PLAN *"OPERATION: KINGFISH"* AND SPENT AS MUCH AS *TEN THOUSAND DOLLARS* ON IT.

THEY TRIED TO CONVINCE ECCENTRIC MILLIONAIRE *HOWARD HUGHES* TO PUT UP A *$1 MILLION SIGNING BONUS* FOR LEW AND INVEST IN AN ABA FRANCHISE IN LOS ANGELES SPECIFICALLY *FOR* HIM.

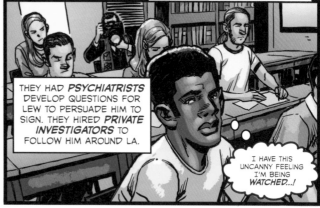

THEY HAD *PSYCHIATRISTS* DEVELOP QUESTIONS FOR LEW TO PERSUADE HIM TO SIGN. THEY HIRED *PRIVATE INVESTIGATORS* TO FOLLOW HIM AROUND LA.

I HAVE THIS UNCANNY FEELING I'M BEING *WATCHED...!*

THE ABA'S RESEARCH SUGGESTED THAT AS MUCH AS LEW RESPECTED HIS **COACH**, JOHN WOODEN, AND HIS **AGENT**, HE WOULD MAKE THE FINAL DECISION **HIMSELF**.

LEW TOLD THE NBA AND THE ABA HE'D BE IN NEW YORK VISITING HIS FOLKS AND HE'D MEET WITH BOTH LEAGUES--**ONCE**.

THEY SHOULD EACH GIVE HIM THEIR **BEST PITCH**, AND **THEN** HE'D MAKE HIS CHOICE.

THE ABA PLOTTED TO BLOW THEIR RIVALS AWAY WITH A **ONE-MILLION-DOLLAR OFFER**.

LEW ALCINDOR
ONE MILLION AND 00/100

GEORGE MIKAN HIMSELF WOULD SHOW UP TO LEW'S HOTEL ROOM AND PRESENT HIM WITH THE CERTIFIED CHECK.

BUT WHEN MIKAN EMERGED FROM THE MEETING WITH LEW:

WE DECIDED THAT IT WASN'T **NECESSARY** TO GIVE HIM OUR BEST OFFER.

WE FIGURE WHEN HE COMES **BACK** TO US, THEN WE'LL USE THE CHECK FOR THE **SECOND** ROUND OF TALKS.

YOU DID **WHAT?**

OF COURSE, TRUE TO HIS WORD, LEW MADE SURE THERE WOULDN'T **BE** A SECOND ROUND.

THE MILWAUKEE BUCKS OF THE NBA MADE THE **BETTER** OFFER (SANS THE $1M CHECK THAT NEVER LEFT MIKAN'S **POCKET**) AND HE SIGNED WITH **THEM**.

MIKAN WAS (RIGHTLY) BLAMED FOR THE ALCINDOR DISASTER.

WHEN THE OWNERS MOVED THE ABA OFFICE TO NEW YORK NOT LONG THEREAFTER, MIKAN AGAIN REFUSED TO LEAVE MINNEAPOLIS AND SO STEPPED DOWN AS COMMISSIONER.

ONCE IN THE NBA, LEW BECAME AN INSTANT SUPERSTAR, WINNING *ROOKIE OF THE YEAR* TO NO ONE'S SURPRISE.

ALWAYS ACTIVE IN POLITICAL CAUSES, WHILE AT SCHOOL LEW *REFUSED* TO REPRESENT AMERICA IN THE OLYMPICS AND JOINED A GROUP OF ATHLETES SUPPORTING *MUHAMMAD ALI*, WHO HAD BEEN BANNED FROM BOXING FOR REFUSING TO SERVE IN THE VIETNAM WAR.

THE POLITICAL UPHEAVALS OF THE 1960S HAD *ALIENATED* HIM FROM THE CATHOLIC CHURCH IN WHICH HE'D BEEN RAISED. HE BEGAN STUDYING THE QURAN WHILE STILL AT UCLA.

AFTER LEADING THE BUCKS TO THE 1971 NBA CHAMPIONSHIP, HE FOLLOWED HEROES ALI AND MALCOM X IN CONVERTING TO *ISLAM* AND TAKING AN ARABIC NAME.

كريم

Kareem
(the noble one)

عبد الجبار

Abdul-Jabbar
(servant of the Almighty)

ABDUL-JABBAR WOULD GO ON TO BECOME THE GREATEST OFFENSIVE PLAYER IN NBA HISTORY, HOLDING THE *ALL-TIME SCORING RECORD* ACROSS HIS TWENTY-YEAR CAREER.

ABDUL-JABBAR WAS SO DOMINANT IN THE NBA THAT THE LEAGUE WAS FORCED TO ABOLISH ONE OF NAISMITH'S ORIGINAL RULES: THE JUMP BALL AFTER *EVERY BASKET*.

OBVIOUSLY, THIS GROUND THE GAME TO A HALT AND RESULTED IN LESS SCORING.

THE NCAA GOT RID OF THAT RULE IN 1937, BUT *RETAINED* THE JUMP AT THE *BEGINNING OF EACH QUARTER*.

CELTICS COACH RED AUERBACH WAS FRUSTRATED THAT THE NOW-LAKER KAREEM ABDUL-JABBAR WOULD WIN EVERY JUMP.

SO RED LOBBIED THE LEAGUE TO DO AWAY WITH THE JUMP *AFTER* THE FIRST QUARTER:

LOOK, THE REFEREES AREN'T VERY *GOOD* AT THROWING THE BALL UP *STRAIGHT*...

...SO LET'S TAKE THE *LUCK* OUT OF IT AND JUST HAVE THEM DO IT JUST *ONCE A NIGHT*.

"THEY *WENT* FOR IT," RED REMEMBERED.

"SO INSTEAD OF THE LAKERS GETTING *FOUR* GUARANTEED POSSESSIONS AT THE START OF QUARTERS, *THEY* GOT TWO AND *WE* GOT TWO."

OOPS.

THIS IS LIKE THE *DUNK* ALL OVER AGAIN!

THE NCAA FINALLY CAME TO ITS SENSES AND LIFTED THE DUNK BAN IN 1976.

THE **ABA** WOULD HAVE NEVER EVEN **CONSIDERED** A DUNK BAN--BECAUSE EVEN WITHOUT ABDUL-JABBAR, THEY HAD A **SUPERSTAR** OF THEIR OWN.

YOUNG **JULIUS ERVING** LEARNED TO PLAY HOOPS ON THE PLAYGROUND COURTS OF NEW YORK...

...WHERE STREET-BALL LEGEND **JUMPIN' JACKIE JACKSON** WOULD RUN THE LENGTH OF THE COURT, TAKE OFF FROM THE FOUL LINE, AND SLAM THE BALL INTO THE HOOP.

JUMPING JACKIE EARNED HIS NICKNAME--HE COULD TAKE A **QUARTER** OFF THE TOP OF THE BACKBOARD!

ERVING EMULATED JACKIE AND QUICKLY BECAME KNOWN AS A **MASTER OF THE DUNK.** AFTER COLLEGE STARDOM AT THE UNIVERSITY OF MASSACHUSETTS, HE WAS DRAFTED BY THE ABA'S VIRGINIA SQUIRES.

IN SQUIRES TRAINING CAMP, WHENEVER ERVING CAME UP WITH A NEW WRINKLE ON THE MOVE, TEAMMATE WILLIE SOJOURNER WOULD SAY:

THERE'S THE **DOCTOR** DIGGING INTO HIS NEW **BAG** AGAIN!

ERVING HAD BEEN KNOWN AS *"THE DOCTOR"* SINCE HIGH SCHOOL.

"DR. J" LED THE ABA IN OFFENSIVE REBOUNDS IN HIS FIRST YEAR WITH VIRGINIA.

TRADED TO THE **NEW YORK NETS,** THE PERENNIAL ALL-STAR LED THE TEAM TO THEIR FIRST ABA TITLE IN 1974.

THE 1976 ABA ALL-STAR TEAM WASN'T EXACTLY A **POWER-HOUSE EVENT**--THERE WERE ONLY **SEVEN** TEAMS IN THE LEAGUE AT THAT POINT, SO THEY DECIDED TO HAVE PLAYERS FROM **SIX** TEAMS PLAY THE HOST, THE **DENVER NUGGETS.**

★ 1ST ANNUAL ★
SLAM DUNK
★★★ CONTEST ★★★
★ THOMPSON ★ ERVING ★
★ GILMORE GERVIN KENON ★
McNICHOLS SPORTS ARENA, DENVER
JAN 27, 1976

BUT IT DID HAVE A **SIDE EVENT** THAT TYPIFIED THE TOTALLY-IN-YOUR-FACE ABA STYLE--THE **SLAM DUNK CONTEST.**

THE WINNER WOULD GET A THOUSAND BUCKS AND A STEREO.

"AS THE CONTEST BEGAN, I HAD A *PLAN*," ERVING REMEMBERED.

"I DID WHAT I CALL THE *IRON CROSS* (FROM MY LEFT SIDE). I'D JUMP BY THE BASKET, SPREAD MY ARMS AS IF I WERE FLYING, THEN DUNK THE BALL BEHIND ME WITHOUT EVER LOOKING AT THE ROOM.

"FOR MY STANDSTILL DUNK UNDER THE BASKET, I TOOK A BASKETBALL IN EACH HAND AND THEN SLAMMED ONE AFTER THE OTHER."

"FOR MY DUNK FROM THE RIGHT SIDE, I DROVE UNDER THE BASKET, GRABBED THE RIM WITH MY RIGHT ARM, AND SLAMMED THE BALL WITH MY LEFT."

DENVER GENERAL MANAGER CARL SCHEER REMEMBERED, "JULIUS WENT TO THE FOUL LINE, *TURNED*, AND STARTED *PACING OFF* IN THE OPPOSITE DIRECTION FROM THE BASKET.

"AS HE PACED OFF, THE CROWD STARTED *SCREAMING*. THEN, WHEN HE GOT TO ABOUT THREE-QUARTERS COURT AND TURNED AND FACED THE BASKET...

"...THERE WAS *SILENCE*.

"THE CROWD KNEW IT WAS GOING TO SEE SOMETHING *SPECIAL*."

THUD

THUD

THUD

"ONLY WHEN THE BALL HIT THE FLOOR DID THE CROWD REACT," SCHEER RECALLED.

BANG

DENVER'S DOUG MOE COMPLAINED JOKINGLY THAT DR. J'S FOOT HAD TOUCHED THE FOUL LINE--AN ILLEGAL LAUNCH.

LOOK, I'M NOT DOING THAT AGAIN!

SPOILER ALERT:

DR. J WON THE STEREO.

WHOA.

NEW YORK NETS ANNOUNCER JOHN STERLING DECLARED, "I CAN SAY WITHOUT A DOUBT THAT WHAT FINALLY CONVINCED THE NBA TO MERGE WAS A CHANCE TO GET *JULIUS* IN THE *LEAGUE*."

THE NBA FINALLY *GAVE IN* AND BROUGHT ABA FRANCHISES INDIANA PACERS, DENVER NUGGETS, NEW YORK NETS, AND SAN ANTONIO SPURS INTO THE LEAGUE.

CONDESCENDING TO THE END, THE NBA REFUSED TO CALL THIS A *"MERGER"*-- INSISTING INSTEAD IT WAS AN *"EXTENSION."*

THE NBA ADOPTED MOST OF THE YOUNGER LEAGUE'S INNOVATIONS--THE 3-POINTER, THE SLAM DUNK--BUT NOT THE TRICOLOR BALL.

"THE (NBA) WAS RUN LIKE *GARBAGE*," COMPLAINED NUGGETS COACH DOUG MOE. "THERE WAS NO *CAMARADERIE*; A LOT OF THE NBA GUYS WERE ALOOF AND THOUGHT THEY WERE TOO GOOD TO PRACTICE OR PLAY HARD."

"*NOW*, THE NBA IS LIKE THE *OLD* ABA.

"HELL, THE ABA MIGHT HAVE LOST THE *BATTLE*...

"...BUT WE *WON* THE *WAR*."

GENEALOGY OF

NBL FRANCHISES

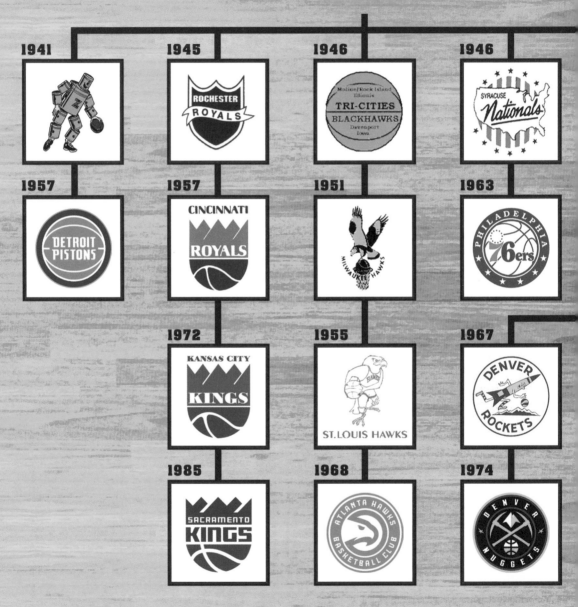

1941

1945 ROCHESTER ROYALS

1946 Moline/Rock Island Illinois TRI-CITIES BLACKHAWKS Davenport Iowa

1946 SYRACUSE Nationals

1957 DETROIT PISTONS

1957 CINCINNATI ROYALS

1951 MILWAUKEE HAWKS

1963 PHILADELPHIA 76ers

1972 KANSAS CITY KINGS

1955 ST. LOUIS HAWKS

1967 DENVER ROCKETS

1985 SACRAMENTO KINGS

1968 ATLANTA HAWKS BASKETBALL CLUB

1974 DENVER NUGGETS

NBA TEAMS

BAA FRANCHISES

1947 MPLS. LAKERS

1946 NEW YORK KNICKS

1946 BOSTON CELTICS

1946 Warriors

1960 LOS ANGELES LAKERS

1962 SAN FRANCISCO WARRIORS

ABA FRANCHISES

1967 CHAPARRALS

1967 INDIANA PACERS

1967 N.J. AMERICANS

1971 GOLDEN STATE WARRIORS

1973 SAN ANTONIO SPURS

1968 NY Nets

1977 New Jersey Nets

2012 NETS B BROOKLYN

EXPANSION

1961

1967 SEATTLE SUPERSONICS

1967 san diego ROCKETS N.B.A.

1970 Buffalo Braves

1962 Zephyrs

2008 THUNDER OKC

1971 HOUSTON ROCKETS

1978 SAN DIEGO Clippers

1963 BALTIMORE Bullets

1984 CLIPPERS

1973 CAPITAL bullets

1966 CHICAGO BULLS

1968 PHOENIX SUNS

1997 WASHINGTON WIZARDS

1980 DALLAS MAVERICKS

1988 MIAMI HEAT

FRANCHISES

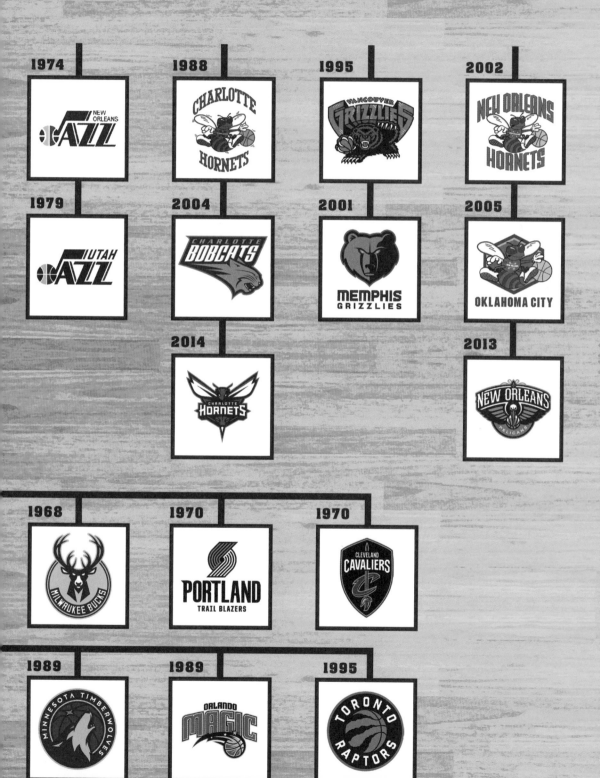

1974 — NEW ORLEANS JAZZ

1988 — CHARLOTTE HORNETS

1995 — VANCOUVER GRIZZLIES

2002 — NEW ORLEANS HORNETS

1979 — UTAH JAZZ

2004 — CHARLOTTE BOBCATS

2001 — MEMPHIS GRIZZLIES

2005 — OKLAHOMA CITY

2014 — CHARLOTTE HORNETS

2013 — NEW ORLEANS PELICANS

1968 — MILWAUKEE BUCKS

1970 — PORTLAND TRAIL BLAZERS

1970 — CLEVELAND CAVALIERS

1989 — MINNESOTA TIMBERWOLVES

1989 — ORLANDO MAGIC

1995 — TORONTO RAPTORS

CHAPTER SIX
MAD MARCH

UNTIL THE 1970S, AMERICAN COLLEGES SPENT ABOUT *1 PERCENT* OF THEIR ANNUAL ATHLETIC BUDGETS ON *WOMEN'S* SPORTS.

THEN, IN 1972, CONGRESS PASSED *AMENDMENTS* TO VARIOUS EDUCATION ACTS, *TITLE IX* OF WHICH PREVENTED ANY EDUCATIONAL PROGRAM THAT RECEIVED *FEDERAL FUNDING* FROM DISCRIMINATING AGAINST STUDENTS ON THE BASIS OF *GENDER*.

CONGRESSMAN *JOHN TOWER* (R-TX) TRIED AND FAILED TO GET *ATHLETIC* PROGRAMS EXCLUDED FROM TITLE IX.

THAT FIGHT LED MANY TO WRONGLY THINK OF TITLE IX AS A *SPORTS* LAW AND NOT AS THE *CIVIL RIGHTS* LAW THAT IT IS, BUT THERE YOU GO.

NO GIRLS ALLOWED

PRIOR TO TITLE IX, SMALLER, *ALL-FEMALE* COLLEGES HAD DOMINATED WOMEN'S BASKETBALL.

THE MIGHTY MACS OF TINY IMMACULATA COLLEGE IN PENNSYLVANIA IMPROBABLY DOMINATED THE WOMEN'S CHAMPIONSHIP FROM 1972 TO 1974, AND THE ENTIRE TEAM WOULD BE INDUCTED INTO THE NAISMITH HALL OF FAME IN 2014.

THE "MACKIES" OF THE SMALL CATHOLIC SCHOOL PRAYED TO THE "GOD OF PLAYERS" BEFORE EVERY GAME.

THEY OFTEN PLAYED THEIR HOME GAMES AT OTHER CAMPUSES BECAUSE THEIR GYM DIDN'T HAVE ANY BLEACHERS...

...BUT THE IMMACULATA SISTERS WOULD ALWAYS PACK THE STANDS TO CHEER ON THEIR MACKIES!

GO MACS

PIONEERING COACH CATHY RUSH MOVED HER TEAMS OFF THE ZONE DEFENSE THAT HAD DOMINATED SINCE THE DAYS OF CLARA BAER AND INSTEAD TAUGHT MAN-TO-MAN DEFENSE THAT REVOLUTIONIZED THE WOMEN'S GAME.

BUT WHEN ENFORCEMENT OF TITLE IX BEGAN IN 1974, THE EFFECTS ON SMALLER PROGRAMS WERE FELT ALMOST IMMEDIATELY.

GO MA

THE ENTRY OF DEEP-POCKETED UNIVERSITIES DOOMED WOMEN'S COLLEGES' DOMINANCE OF THE SPORT, AS THEY COULDN'T KEEP UP WITH THE BIG SCHOOLS IN RECRUITING TALENT.

UCLA

IN 1974, ANN MEYERS, A SEVEN-LETTER SPORTSWOMAN IN HIGH SCHOOL, BECAME THE FIRST WOMAN TO SIGN A FOUR-YEAR ATHLETIC SCHOLARSHIP SO SHE COULD PLAY BASKETBALL FOR UCLA.

AS A GUIDANCE COUNSELOR IN MASSACHUSETTS, *RUTHANN LOBO* KNEW WHAT HER DAUGHTER *REBECCA*'S RIGHTS WERE UNDER *TITLE IX* IN ITS EARLY DAYS.

WHEN THE HEAD OF PARKS AND REC CALLED TO TELL HER THAT ONLY REBECCA AND ONE OTHER GIRL HAD SIGNED UP FOR BASKETBALL THAT SEASON, RUTHANN POINTED OUT THAT UNDER THE LAW, THE FOURTH GRADER COULD PLAY ON THE *BOYS'* TEAM INSTEAD. SHE SAID:

"WHEN YOU YELL AT *THEM*, YOU YELL AT *HER*.

"WHEN *THEY* RUN SPRINTS, *SHE* RUNS SPRINTS.

EVERYTHING NEEDS TO BE THE *SAME*.

EXCEPT WHEN YOU SCRIMMAGE SHIRTS AND SKINS. THEN I WANT HER ON THE *SHIRTS'* TEAM.

AT AGE *TEN*, HOOPS-MAD REBECCA WROTE *RED AUERBACH* DECLARING THAT ONE DAY SHE WOULD BE HIS FIRST *FEMALE* CELTIC.

(HER *GRANDMOTHER* DELIVERED IT TO BOSTON'S GENERAL MANAGER IN PERSON!)

THOUGH SHE WAS AT THE HEAD OF THE TEAM AS THEY TOOK THE COURT, SUANNE DIDN'T DRIBBLE TO THE BASKET AND TAKE A PRACTICE SHOT.

SHE DRAPED HER WARM-UP JACKET AROUND HER SHOULDERS AND BEGAN PERFORMING A TRADITIONAL *LAKOTA SHAWL DANCE*.

"ALL THAT STUFF THE LEAD FANS WERE YELLING--IT WAS LIKE SHE *REVERSED* IT SOMEHOW," A TEAMMATE SAID.

INSTEAD, SHE STOOD ALONE AT CENTER COURT AND FACED THE LEAD FANS.

THE CATCALLS TURNED INTO SILENCE...

...AND THEN TO *CHEERS*.

DO WE NEED TO EVEN TELL YOU THAT PINE RIDGE *WON THE GAME?*

AS SHE MATURED INTO A BONA FIDE HIGH SCHOOL BASKETBALL STAR, SUANNE COULD DREAM OF CONVERTING HER SKILLS INTO A SCHOLARSHIP TO HELP HER GET *OUT* OF PINE RIDGE...

...JUST AS **BOYS** FROM MIDDLE- AND LOWER-CLASS FAMILIES HAD DONE FOR DECADES BEFORE HER.

EARVIN JOHNSON GREW UP IN A WORKING-CLASS AREA OF LANSING, MICHIGAN, WHERE HIS FATHER WORKED MULTIPLE JOBS--AND HIS MOTHER WORKED AS A SCHOOL JANITOR--TO SUPPORT HIS SIX SIBLINGS (AND THREE HALF-SIBLINGS).

LARRY BIRD CAME FROM THE POOREST FAMILY IN THE POOREST COUNTY IN INDIANA, IN A TOWN CALLED FRENCH LICK.

BUSSED FROM HIS PREDOMINANTLY BLACK NEIGHBOR-HOOD TO A LARGELY WHITE SCHOOL BECAUSE OF **DESEGREGATION**, JOHNSON FOUND HIMSELF ABLE TO MIX WITH PEOPLE VASTLY DIFFERENT THAN HIMSELF.

A LOCAL REPORTER NICKNAMED HIM **"MAGIC"** AS MUCH FOR HIS AMAZING **PERSONALITY** AS FOR HIS **COURT SKILLS.**

BIRD WAS SO **SHY** AND WITHDRAWN THAT HE REFUSED TO ATTEND HIS OLDER BROTHER'S CHAMPIONSHIP BASKETBALL GAME BECAUSE HE HATED CROWDS.

HE FLUNKED ENGLISH ONE YEAR BECAUSE HE REFUSED TO GIVE A **SPEECH** BEFORE THE CLASS.

IN HIS SENIOR YEAR, MAGIC LED EVERETT HIGH SCHOOL TO A 27-1 RECORD AND AVERAGED **28.8** POINTS A GAME...

...WHILE LARRY AVERAGED **31 POINTS** AS THE ALL-TIME SCORER FOR SPRINGS VALLEY HIGH.

AS BOTH BOYS NEARED GRADUATION, THE **COLLEGE RECRUITERS** STARTED SWARMING. SO **MANY** SHOWED UP ON HIS DOORSTEP, MAGIC BEGAN HIDING OUT AT FRIENDS' HOUSES.

THE PHONE RANG SO **INCESSANTLY** THAT THE JOHNSONS HAD TO CHANGE THEIR NUMBER.

TORN BY HIS DECISION ABOUT WHICH SCHOOL TO GO TO, MAGIC VISITED **EARVIN SENIOR** ON HIS LATE SHIFT AT A LOCAL BODY SHOP.

I KNOW YOU WANT ME TO GO TO **MICHIGAN STATE.**

YEAH, I'D **LIKE** YOU TO GO THERE BECAUSE IT'S CLOSE AND WE'LL GET TO SEE YOU.

BUT WHEREVER YOU GO, WE'RE GOING TOO. IT'S ALL ON YOU, JUNIOR.

EXCITEMENT WAS **SO** INTENSE ABOUT THE POSSIBILITY OF THE LOCAL HERO COMING TO PLAY FOR MSU THAT MAGIC'S PRESS CONFERENCE TO ANNOUNCE HIS DECISION WAS PUMPED THROUGH THE SCHOOL'S LOUDSPEAKERS.

UM, NEXT YEAR I WILL BE, UH, ATTENDING MICHIGAN STATE UNIVERSITY...

BIRD WAS **ALSO** RECRUITED BY A LOCAL NCAA POWERHOUSE, **INDIANA UNIVERSITY.** HE HAD BEEN PERSONALLY COURTED BY THE PROGRAM'S TEMPESTUOUS HEAD COACH, **BOBBY KNIGHT.**

"THE GENERAL" WAS NOT EVEN *HALFWAY THROUGH* HIS LEGENDARY RUN WITH THE HOOSIERS, WHICH HE WOULD COACH UNTIL 2000.

IN THAT TIME, THE CHAIR-THROWING FIREBRAND WOULD BRING THE SCHOOL ONE NIT AND *THREE* NCAA CHAMPIONSHIPS, ALONG WITH *ELEVEN* BIG TEN CROWNS.

HE'D ALSO BE THE SUBJECT OF ONE OF THE MOST FAMOUS BASKETBALL BOOKS OF ALL TIME, *A SEASON ON THE BRINK* BY JOHN FEINSTEIN, IN WHICH THE SPORTSWRITER FOLLOWED THE IU HOOSIERS FOR THE ENTIRE 1985–86 SEASON.

WHEN THE STAR *COACH* PASSED HIS STAR *FRESHMAN* ON CAMPUS IN THE FIRST MONTH OF SCHOOL, THOUGH...

...KNIGHT WALKED RIGHT *PAST* BIRD WITHOUT RECOGNIZING HIM!

THE INCIDENT SUMMED UP LARRY'S INITIAL COLLEGE EXPERIENCE.

LARRY FOUND IU UTTERLY OVERWHELMING—THE UNIVERSITY HAD *30,000* STUDENTS, *SIX TIMES* THE ENTIRE POPULATION OF FRENCH LICK!

AM I SKIPPING LUNCH OR DINNER TODAY?

THOUGH HE HAD A FULL BASKET-BALL SCHOLARSHIP, BIRD WAS STILL *POOR*, AND STILL *BROKE*.

WHEN THE INDIANA ATHLETIC PROGRAM WOULDN'T REIMBURSE HIM A *$60 FEE* FOR A BOWLING CLASS, HE DECIDED HE HAD SEEN ALL OF COLLEGE THAT HE *NEEDED* TO.

INCREDIBLY, THE ONE-TIME GUARANTEED SUPERSTAR JOINED A *STREET CREW* IN FRENCH LICK, PICKING UP BRUSH, MOWING LAWNS, AND COLLECTING GARBAGE.

RECRUITERS FROM INDIANA UNIVERSITY RIVAL *INDIANA STATE*, HEARING OF BIRD'S DROPPING OUT, DROVE TO FRENCH LICK TO TALK TO HIM...

...BUT HE WASN'T *HOME*. SO THEY DROVE AROUND TOWN UNTIL THEY FOUND HIM HELPING HIS GRANDMOTHER OUT OF A LAUNDROMAT.

AT FIRST HE SAID HE DIDN'T WANT TO TALK TO THEM, BUT HIS GRAND-MOTHER *INSISTED*.

THE TALK IN GRANDMA BIRD'S LIVING ROOM TURNED TOWARD A TALENTED LOCAL ASSISTANT COACH WHO NEVER WENT TO UNIVERSITY.

HE WOULD HAVE BEEN A REALLY GOOD PLAYER IF HE HAD GONE TO COLLEGE.

YOU KNOW, LARRY...

...SOMEDAY THEY'RE GONNA SAY THE SAME THING ABOUT *YOU* IF YOU DON'T GO TO SCHOOL.

WHAT ARE YOU GOING TO DO, WORK ON A GARBAGE TRUCK YOUR WHOLE LIFE?

I DON'T KNOW, IT'S A PRETTY GOOD JOB. I LIKE IT."

MAYBE HE WAS PLAYING *HARD TO GET*, BUT EVENTUALLY BIRD AGREED TO PLAY FOR THE *ISU SYCAMORES.*

BIRD REWARDED ISU'S PURSUIT WITH ALMOST *PATHOLOGICAL PRACTICING* AND *STELLAR PLAY*.

OTHER TEAMS TRIED TO DEVELOP A *"BIRD CAGE"* DEFENSE BY PUTTING A TRIANGLE AND TWO ROVERS ON HIM--

--BUT HE COUNTERED THIS STRATEGY BY DRAWING AWAY THE *DEFENDERS* AND LETTING *FREE PLAYERS* MAKE SHOTS.

IN HIS SENIOR YEAR, HE LED TERRA HAUTE TO AN UNDEFEATED RECORD, EARNING A BERTH TO THE NCAA CHAMPIONSHIPS--THE ANNUAL *"MARCH MADNESS"* AT THE END OF EVERY WINTER.

THE MADNESS OF MARCH IS RUNNING./THE WINGED FEET FLY, THE BALL SAILS HIGH...

THOUGH NOW ASSOCIATED EXCLUSIVELY WITH *COLLEGE* BALL, THE PHRASE WAS POPULARIZED BY HENRY V. PORTER, ASSISTANT EXECUTIVE SECRETARY OF THE ILLINOIS *HIGH SCHOOL* ASSOCIATION IN A POEM FOR THE *ILLINOIS INTERSCHOLASTIC* IN 1942.

CHICAGO-AREA SPORTSCASTER *BRENT MUSBURGER* IS CREDITED WITH APPLYING THE PHRASE TO THE NCAA TOURNEY ON ESPN IN THE EARLY 1980S.

ONCE A MERE EIGHT TEAMS, BY 1979 THE TOURNAMENT INVOLVED *FORTY*, WHITTLED DOWN, OVER THE COURSE OF THE MONTH, TO THE *"SWEET SIXTEEN"*...THE *"ELITE EIGHT"*...THE *"FINAL FOUR"*...

~~Penn~~

Michigan State

Michigan State

Indiana State

Indiana State

~~De Paul~~

...UNTIL AT LAST, ONLY LARRY BIRD'S SYCAMORES WERE LEFT...

...FACING MICHIGAN STATE AND *EARVIN JOHNSON*.

Sports Illustrated

THE SUPER SOPHS

MAGIC WAS COLLEGE HOOPS' *GREATEST STAR*, HAVING LED THE SPARTANS TO THE ELITE EIGHT THE YEAR BEFORE AND GRACING THE COVER OF *SPORTS ILLUSTRATED*.

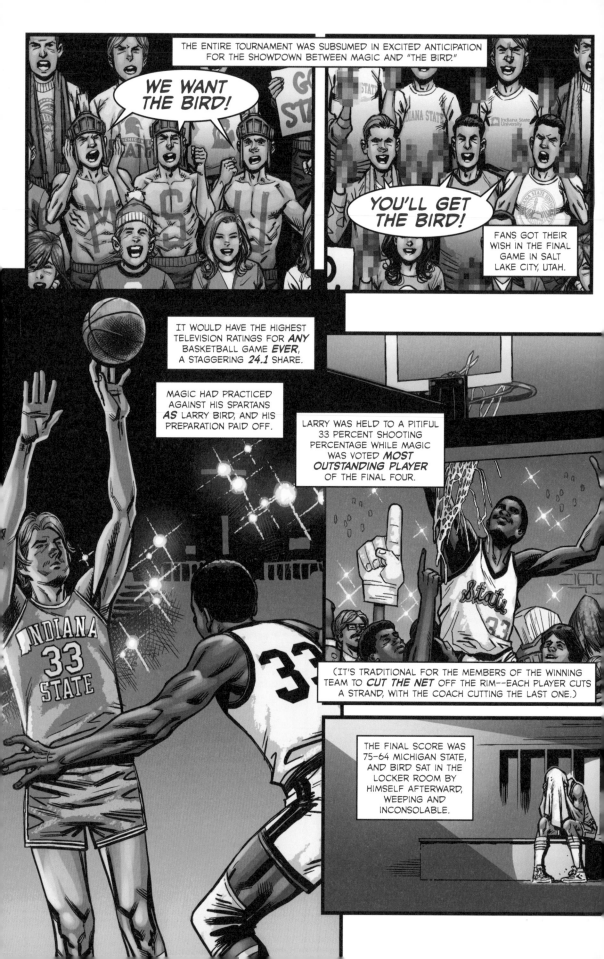

CBS SPORTS

NCAA

EVEN THOUGH THE MUCH-HYPED SHOWDOWN WASN'T MUCH OF A *GAME*, IT SOLIDIFIED THE STATUS OF MARCH MADNESS AS ONE OF AMERICA'S PREMIER ANNUAL SPORTING EVENTS.

IN 1981, CBS POACHED THE NCAA FROM NBC FOR *$48 MILLION* OVER THE NEXT THREE YEARS.

THE NETWORK WAS REWARDED THE FOLLOWING YEAR, WITH ANOTHER THRILLING *FINAL FOUR*, IN THE SUPERDOME IN NEW ORLEANS.

UNIVERSITY OF NORTH CAROLINA'S *MICHAEL JORDAN* HIT THE CHAMPIONSHIP-WINNING SHOT TO BEAT *PATRICK EWING*'S GEORGETOWN.

MAGIC AND LARRY'S COMPETITION CONTINUED INTO THEIR NBA SIGNINGS--BIRD JUST EDGED JOHNSON'S $500,000 BONUS WITH THE LOS ANGELES LAKERS WITH HIS OWN *$600,000* PAYDAY FROM THE BOSTON CELTICS.

A KID WHO HAD TO DROP OUT OF SCHOOL OVER A *$60 BOWLING FEE* HAD JUST SIGNED A FIVE-YEAR, *$3.25 MILLION* CONTRACT--THE RICHEST FOR A *ROOKIE* IN BASKETBALL HISTORY.

3.3
3.1
3.0
1.0
0

MAGIC   BIRD

EVERYONE WHO PLAYS COLLEGE BALL *DREAMS* OF THAT KIND OF A PAYDAY...BUT ONLY A SELECT *FEW* ACHIEVE IT.

COLLEGE SPORTS IS *BIG BUSINESS*, A MAJOR SOURCE OF REVENUE AND THE INSPIRATION FOR COUNTLESS *DONATIONS* FROM ALUMNI.

BUT FOR ALL THE MONEY THEY GENERATE FOR A SCHOOL, STUDENT-ATHLETES ARE NOT THEMSELVES *PAID*-- NOR ARE THEY ALLOWED TO *UNIONIZE*.

THEIR *COACHES*, HOWEVER, MAKE *MILLIONS* WHILE CONTROLLING THE DESTINIES OF THEIR YOUNG PLAYERS.

THE MOST RECENT STATISTICS SUGGEST THAT BARELY *ONE IN SEVENTY-FIVE* NCAA MEN'S PLAYERS GET DRAFTED BY THE NBA...

HELLO?

...THAT'S *1.3 PERCENT.*

SCHOOLS CLAIM, OF COURSE, THAT ATHLETES RECEIVE FREE TUITION AND OTHER BENEFITS THAT WILL PROVE OF VALUE EVEN IF THEY DON'T GO PRO.

BUT A RECENT REPORT FROM THE INSTITUTE FOR DIVERSITY AND ETHICS IN SPORT FOUND THAT ONLY *78 PERCENT* OF MALE NCAA TOURNAMENT BASKETBALL PLAYERS EVEN *GRADUATE!*

WOMEN PLAYERS DO CONSIDERABLY BETTER, AT 92 PERCENT. (AND IT MUST BE SAID ATHLETIC PROGRAMS DO CONSIDERABLY BETTER THAN THE NATIONAL COLLEGE GRADUATION RATE OF *60 PERCENT.*)

THE NCAA HAD ORIGINALLY LOBBIED *AGAINST* TITLE IX OUT OF FEAR THAT IT WOULD DRAIN FUNDS FROM MEN'S PROGRAMS. BUT THE ORGANIZATION SOON REALIZED *WOMEN'S* SPORTS COULD BE LUCRATIVE TOO.

SINCE 1971, THE WOMEN'S BASKETBALL CHAMPIONSHIPS HAD BEEN ORGANIZED BY THE ASSOCIATION FOR INTERCOLLEGIATE ATHLETICS FOR WOMEN (AIAW).

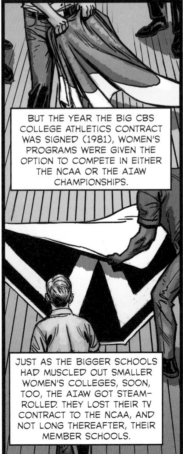

BUT THE YEAR THE BIG CBS COLLEGE ATHLETICS CONTRACT WAS SIGNED (1981), WOMEN'S PROGRAMS WERE GIVEN THE OPTION TO COMPETE IN EITHER THE NCAA OR THE AIAW CHAMPIONSHIPS.

JUST AS THE BIGGER SCHOOLS HAD MUSCLED OUT SMALLER WOMEN'S COLLEGES, SOON, TOO, THE AIAW GOT STEAM-ROLLED. THEY LOST THEIR TV CONTRACT TO THE NCAA, AND NOT LONG THEREAFTER, THEIR MEMBER SCHOOLS.

THE AIAW FILED AN ANTITRUST LAWSUIT AGAINST THE NCAA IN 1982, BUT WHEN THE COURTS RULED AGAINST THEM, THE ORGANIZATION WENT THE WAY OF THE DINOSAURS AND THE NCAA ABSORBED THEIR FUNCTIONS.

WOMEN JOINED MEN IN THE ANNUAL *MARCH MADNESS.* TODAY, THE WOMEN'S FINAL GAME IS PLAYED THE DAY AFTER THE MEN'S.

NOW IMPOVERISHED *GIRLS* COULD DREAM OF GOING TO COLLEGE FOR *FREE* THANKS TO THEIR ATHLETIC SKILLS, JUST LIKE THE BIRDS AND MAGICS OF THE WORLD.

IN THE LAST ELEVEN SECONDS OF THE SOUTH DAKOTA CHAMPIONSHIP GAME AGAINST MILBANK HIGH SCHOOL, SHE GOT AN INBOUNDS PASS, TRIED A JUMP SHOT, MISSED, BUT GOT THE BALL BACK ON THE REBOUND.

BZZZZZZZZZZZT

SHE SANK A BUZZER-BEATER TO WIN THE GAME FOR PINE RIDGE.

FEW PLACES ARE MORE IMPOVER-ISHED IN AMERICA THAN THE *PINE RIDGE INDIAN RESERVATION*, WHERE *SUANNE BIG CROW* HAD EVOLVED INTO A FULL-FLEDGED HIGH SCHOOL BASKETBALL STAR.

THE LADY THORPES RETURNED TO THE "REZ" *HEROES*.

SUANNE HEADLINED A NATIVE AMERICAN WOMEN'S ALL-STAR TEAM THAT TOURED EUROPE AND AUSTRALIA.

RECRUITERS FROM COLUMBIA, COLORADO, AND PENN STATE CAME CALLING TO PERSUADE HER TO COME PLAY DIVISION I BASKETBALL FOR THEM.

BUT IN FEBRUARY 1992, SUANNE HAD TO DRIVE TO HURON FOR SOUTH DAKOTA'S *MISS BASKETBALL* BANQUET.

SHE FELL ASLEEP AT THE WHEEL AND HER CAR RAN OFF THE ROAD.

WHILE HER MOTHER, CHICK, SURVIVED, SUANNE DID NOT.

SHE HAD NOT YET TURNED *EIGHTEEN YEARS OLD*.

A MEDICINE MAN TOLD CHICK THAT SUANNE HAD BEEN THE SPIRIT OF A *GREAT LEADER*, WHO HAD COME BACK TO *REUNITE* THE PEOPLE.

IN 1992, CHICK BIG CROW FOUNDED THE SUANNE BIG CROW BOYS AND GIRLS CLUB AT PINE RIDGE—THE *FIRST* ON A NATIVE AMERICAN RESERVATION.

BY 2013, THERE WERE TWO HUNDRED BOYS AND GIRLS CLUBS ON "REZES" ACROSS THE WEST AND MIDWEST, WHERE PLAYERS COULD DREAM THE DREAM SUANNE WAS *DENIED*.

HOOPS ARE SO BIG ON AMERICAN INDIAN RESERVATIONS THAT IT HAS ITS OWN *"JULY MADNESS,"* THE NATIVE AMERICAN BASKETBALL INVITATIONAL (NABI), WHICH BEGAN IN 2002.

IN JULY 2018, THE NABI TOURNAMENT FEATURED 128 TEAMS, COMPRISING 1,500 HIGH SCHOOLS REPRESENTING MORE THAN 300 TRIBES FROM NORTH AMERICA AND NEW ZEALAND.

GREAT NATIVE AMERICAN NOVELIST AND POET *SHERMAN ALEXIE* HAS SAID, "BASKETBALL, IN THE UNITED STATES AT LEAST, PLAYS THE SAME FUNCTION THAT *SOCCER* DOES EVERYWHERE ELSE IN THE WORLD. IT'S THE SPORT OF *POVERTY*. IT'S THE SPORT BORN OF POVERTY. IT'S THE *CHEAPEST* SPORT."

IT IS THAT *UNIVERSALITY* THAT UNITES A PEOPLE... AND PROVES THE MEDICINE MAN *RIGHT*.

CHAPTER SEVEN
IT'S "SHOWTIME"

MAGIC JOHNSON AND LARRY BIRD ENTERED A PRO LEAGUE WRACKED BY *CONTROVERSY* AND STRUGGLING TO RETAIN FANS.

JOHNSON'S MILLION-WATT *SMILE* SUGGESTED ALL OF THAT WOULD SOON *CHANGE*.

"UNTIL THAT MOMENT, THE NBA WAS--FOR MANY AMERICANS--*BLACK GUYS IN SHORT SHORTS SNORTING COCAINE*," SAID SPORTS REPORTER PAT O'BRIEN. "MAGIC WAS A *SAVIOR*."

THE ROOKIE ARRIVED AT THE LA LAKERS' TRAINING CAMP TO JOIN A TEAM LONG DOMINATED BY ITS TEAM CAPTAIN AND BIGGEST STAR, *KAREEM ABDUL-JABBAR*.

THOUGH WELL ON HIS WAY TO BECOMING THE LEAGUE'S ALL-TIME OFFENSIVE LEADER, ABDUL-JABBAR ALMOST SEEMED TO PRIDE HIMSELF ON HIS...*UNLOVABILITY*.

LONG ANNOYED BY CONSTANT QUESTIONS AND COMMENTS FROM WHITE FANS AND WRITERS ABOUT HIS *HEIGHT*, *RELIGION*, AND *POLITICS*, ABDUL-JABBAR HAD ALL BUT GIVEN UP *SIGNING AUTOGRAPHS*.

MR. JABBAR?

MR. JABBAR?

SIR?

← ✈ Departures → Arrivals ✈

aggage

ggage ↓

ABDUL-JABBAR "ADOPTED" THE ROOKIE AT CAMP, HAZING THE COLLEGE SUPERSTAR BY HAVING MAGIC FETCH HIS *NEW YORK TIMES* AND ORANGE JUICE EVERY MORNING.

BUT THE PLAYING STYLES OF THE VETERAN STAR AND THE UP-AND-COMER SOON CLASHED LIKE *OIL AND WATER.*

IT TOOK EVERYONE A WHILE TO ADJUST TO MAGIC'S UNCANNY *PASSING* ABILITY.

BONK

GRR.

HE COULD PASS TO PLAYERS WHO DIDN'T EVEN REALIZE THEY WERE *OPEN* UNTIL THE BALL WAS IN THEIR HANDS!

ONCE THE SEASON STARTED WITH JOHNSON AS A POINT GUARD, THE LAKERS' EXCITING PLAY VAULTED THEM TO A 60-22 RECORD AND A TRIP TO THE 1980 FINALS, WHERE THEY BATTLED DR. J'S PHILADELPHIA 76ERS.

OFFENSIVE LEADER KAREEM ABDUL-JABBAR AVERAGED 33 POINTS FOR THE FIRST FIVE GAMES, WITH THE LAKERS LEADING 3-2, BUT THEN HE SPRAINED HIS ANKLE IN GAME 5.

JOHNSON STARTED INSTEAD, AND IN THE PROCESS OF PLAYING GUARD, FORWARD, *AND* CENTER DURING GAME 6, HAD 42 POINTS, 15 REBOUNDS, 7 ASSISTS, AND 3 STEALS.

LA WON, 123-107, AND JOHNSON WAS NAMED FINALS MVP--THE FIRST *ROOKIE* SO REWARDED.

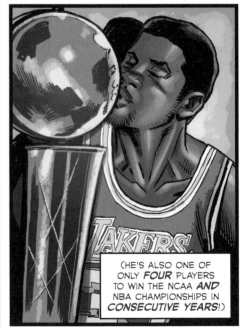

(HE'S ALSO ONE OF ONLY *FOUR* PLAYERS TO WIN THE NCAA *AND* NBA CHAMPIONSHIPS IN *CONSECUTIVE YEARS!*)

IN HIS FIRST YEAR IN LOS ANGELES, MAGIC HAD DONE SOMETHING EVEN THE STORIED ABDUL-JABBAR HAD NOT ACHIEVED IN *HIS ENTIRE TENURE*--WIN THE LAKERS A *CHAMPIONSHIP*.

THERE WAS A SENSE, EVEN IN THAT *EARLY* SERIES, THAT THE TORCH WAS ABOUT TO PASS TO A *NEW GENERATION*.

LAKERS TICKETS SUDDENLY BECAME THE *HOTTEST* IN HOLLYWOOD, AND FOR A TOWN AWASH IN STARDOM, THE PLACE ALL THE STARS WANTED TO *BE* SEEN WAS *COURTSIDE* AT THE *FORUM*.

CANNY OWNER *JERRY BUSS* STARTED THE TRADITION OF PUTTING CELEBRITIES IN THE *FRONT ROW*. THOUGH BUSS'S BACKGROUND WAS IN REAL ESTATE, HE KNEW HOW TO PUT ON A *SHOW*.

HE USED TO FREQUENT A NIGHTCLUB ON WILSHIRE BOULEVARD, WHERE THE ENTERTAINMENT BEGAN WITH A SONG CALLED:

IT'S... *SHOWTIME!*

BUSS HIRED SPANDEX-CLAD "LAKERS GIRLS" AS CHEER-LEADERS AND HAD A NUT NAMED *DANCING BARRY* CUTTING UP THE AISLES.

IN JOHNSON'S SECOND YEAR, NEW COACH (AND FORMER LAKER PLAYER) *PAT RILEY* BECAME AN ICON OF SHARP SUITS AND SHARPER APHORISMS.

TO HAVE LONG-TERM SUCCESS AS A COACH OR IN ANY POSITION OF *LEADERSHIP*, YOU HAVE TO BE *OBSESSED* IN SOME WAY.

RILEY EXPLOITED MAGIC'S PASSING SKILLS AND ABDUL-JABBAR'S SCORING ABILITY FOR A SPECTACULAR *FAST-BREAK STRATEGY* TO OVERWHELM DEFENSES AND SCORE QUICKLY AND OFTEN. THE LAKERS BEAT THE 76ERS AGAIN TO WIN THE 1981 CROWN.

IT WAS A THRILLING BRAND OF BASKET-BALL THAT WAS QUICKLY DUBBED *"SHOWTIME."*

THE AFTER-GAME PARTIES WERE TYPICALLY EXCESSIVE '80S BACCHANALS, FEATURING COCAINE, BOOZE, AND WOMEN.

IN MAGIC'S CASE, THERE WERE A *LOT* OF WOMEN.

FORUM CLUB

HE'D SEE TWO OR THREE GIRLS *BEFORE* PRACTICE, *AFTER* PRACTICE, AND THEN AFTER THE *GAME*.

"EARVIN LOVES WOMEN," SAID MSU STUDENT MANAGER DARWIN PAYTON. "THAT'S HIS ONLY VICE. HE DOESN'T SMOKE. HE DOESN'T DRINK. HE DOESN'T GAMBLE. I'VE NEVER SEEN HIM DRINK A BEER, BUT HE WAS DATING MICHIGAN STATE GIRLS WHEN HE WAS [STILL] IN HIGH SCHOOL."

IT WASN'T ALL GIRLS AND GLORY FOR THE LAKERS.

KAREEM ABDUL-JABBAR'S BEL-AIR MANSION BURNED DOWN IN 1983, ROBBING HIM OF A LIFETIME OF MEMORIES--AND A PRICELESS COLLECTION OF MORE THAN THREE THOUSAND *JAZZ ALBUMS*.

SYMPATHETIC LAKERS FANS WOULD HELP HIM REPLENISH IT BY JUST *GIVING* HIM ALBUMS ON THE ROAD.

MR. JABBAR? THIS IS FOR YOU...!

THANKS, KID...!

THE LAKERS' RISE IN THE NATIONAL CONSCIOUSNESS ALSO HAD MUCH TO DO WITH THE LEAGUE'S DYNAMIC NEW COMMISSIONER, *DANIEL STERN*.

STARTING OUT AS THE LEAGUE'S *LAWYER*, STERN LED THE NBA TO VICTORY WHEN LEGENDARY POINT GUARD *OSCAR ROBERTSON* SUED THEM TO PREVENT THE MERGER WITH THE *ABA* AS A VIOLATION OF ANTITRUST LAWS.

ROBERTSON ARGUED THAT THE NBA'S *OPTION CLAUSE*, WHICH BOUND A DRAFTED PLAYER TO A SINGLE TEAM *IN PERPETUITY* (BARRING A TRADE), CONSTITUTED AN UNFAIR LABOR PRACTICE.

WHUD

SALARY CAP

STERN *SETTLED* THE CASE IN 1976, *ENDING* THE OPTION CLAUSE AND BRINGING *FREE AGENCY* TO THE NBA. PLAYERS COULD SELL THEIR SERVICES TO ANY TEAM ONCE THEY PUT IN ENOUGH SERVICE TIME. THIS *ENRICHED* THEM ASTRONOMICALLY.

BUT STERN ALSO GOT PLAYERS TO AGREE TO A *SALARY CAP* TO LIMIT PLAYERS' SALARIES AND PREVENT RICH TEAMS FROM BUYING THEIR WAY TO THE PLAYOFFS. HE ALSO INSTITUTED *DRUG TESTING* TO CURB RAMPANT COCAINE USE AMONG ITS STARS.

STERN BECAME COMMISSIONER ON *FEBRUARY 1, 1984*, AND WAS ABLE TO PARLEY THE RISE OF SUCH TALENTS AS MAGIC, BIRD, AND JORDAN INTO MASSIVE SUCCESS FOR THE LEAGUE:

DURING HIS TWENTY-YEAR REIGN, STERN EXPANDED THE NBA INTO *THIRTY* TEAMS, A SECOND *COUNTRY* (CANADA), AND A *WORLDWIDE TELEVISION PRESENCE*.

CAP CEILING

LOS ANGELES LAKERS

THE LAKERS DOMINATED THE WESTERN CONFERENCE IN 1983-84--JUST AS THE EAST WAS DOMINATED BY THE BOSTON CELTICS, LED BY JOHNSON'S COLLEGE NEMESIS *LARRY BIRD*.

THAT SEASON'S FINALS WAS QUICKLY DUBBED *"SHOWDOWN '84"* AS IT WOULD BE A REMATCH OF *"MAGIC VERSUS THE BIRD."*

SHOWDOWN '84

RED AUERBACH, THE TEAM'S GENERAL MANAGER, MADE SURE THERE WAS NOTHING *HOSPITABLE* ABOUT BOSTON GARDEN FOR OUT-OF-TOWN PLAYERS. THE VISITORS' LOCKER ROOM WASN'T *CLEANED* AND THE THERMOSTAT WAS KEPT *OFF*.

AUERBACH WOULD HAVE STRANGERS CALL THE PLAYERS' HOTEL ROOMS IN THE MIDDLE OF THE NIGHT, INTERRUPTING THEIR SLEEP.

BBBBRRRIIIIIINNNNNNG

HISTORY WEIGHED HEAVILY ON THE SERIES--DATING BACK TO THEIR DAYS IN MINNEAPOLIS, THE LAKERS HAD FAILED TO DEFEAT THE CELTICS IN *SEVEN* FINALS.

THE NEARLY ALL-BLACK LAKERS WERE NOT NECESSARILY THRILLED TO BE "HIGH NOONING" IT IN BOSTON, A CITY NOTORIOUS FOR ITS *RACIAL ANIMUS*.

THE PLAYERS HAD TO WAIT *FORTY-FIVE* MINUTES AT LOGAN AIRPORT FOR THEIR BAGS, HALF OF WHICH WERE *UNZIPPED*.

HEY MAGIC-- LARRY IS GOING TO MAKE YOU DISAPPEAR!

LARRY IS GONNA *KILL* YOU.

ARE WE GOING TO MAKE IT TO THE HOTEL ALL RIGHT?

AT THE HOTEL, EVERYONE WAS WEARING BIRD'S JERSEY.

HERE'S YOUR **KEY!**

LAKERS RESERVE BOB McADOO HAD SPENT A MISERABLE YEAR AS A CELTIC AND KNEW THERE WAS A **RACIAL** ASPECT TO THE FIERCE IDENTIFICATION OF WORKING-CLASS BOSTON WITH THE RARE **WHITE** NBA SUPERSTAR.

McADOO CALLED THE CITY "A GRAVEYARD FOR BLACKS."

EVER SINCE COLLEGE, BIRD HAD HAD TO DEAL WITH THE "GREAT WHITE HOPE" MANTLE THROWN ON HIM. IT MADE HIM EXTREMELY UNCOMFORTABLE...

I'M NOT A RACIST, BUT THERE AREN'T THAT MANY WHITES LEFT BECAUSE THERE ARE SO MANY GOOD, GREAT BLACK PLAYERS.

I HOPE I CAN HOLD MYSELF UP WITH THEM. I KNOW THEY'RE WAITING FOR ME.

(...BUT THEN, EVERYTHING EXCEPT BEING ON THE **COURT** MADE LARRY BIRD UNCOMFORTABLE.)

LARRY ENTERED HIS FIRST TRAINING CAMP WITH HIS MOSTLY BLACK TEAMMATES DOUBTING A WHITE MAN COULD GIVE THEM ANY SERIOUS COMPETITION--BUT THEY LEFT THAT FIRST PRACTICE EXTREMELY IMPRESSED.

DAMN THIS WHITE GUY CAN PLAY!

BOSTON IMMEDIATELY RALLIED AROUND THE BLUE-COLLAR, ROUGH-EDGED BIRD WHO PLAYED, AS HE SAID...

...LIKE EVERYONE ELSE IN THE WORLD WAS **AGAINST** ME.

HE DIDN'T MIND PEOPLE WATCHING HIM MOW HIS OWN LAWN AT HIS NEW ENGLAND HOUSE, A SATURDAY RITUAL THAT GARNERED *HUGE CROWDS*.

BIRD NEVER FORGOT--OR *FORGAVE*--LOSING TO MAGIC IN THE NCAA TITLE GAME. LARRY FOULED HIM HARD IN THEIR FIRST NBA MEETING.

IT WAS *BIRD*, NOT MAGIC, WHO WAS NAMED *ROOKIE OF THE YEAR* IN 1980. JOHNSON WAS SUFFICIENTLY INSPIRED TO RALLY THE LAKERS TO A *CHAMPIONSHIP* LATER THAT SAME NIGHT.

THE FOLLOWING SEASON, LARRY FOUND HIMSELF OBSESSIVELY CHECKING NEWSPAPER BOX SCORES TO SEE *JOHNSON'S* STATS FOR THE PREVIOUS NIGHT'S GAME.

!#$%@ *EARVIN!*

"IT WAS LIKE A CRUTCH," HE SAID, "[HAVING] SOMEONE TO COMPARE MYSELF TO."

MAGIC WAS INCREASINGLY ANNOYED THAT THE SPORTSWRITER INTELLIGENTSIA SAID HE COULD CONTROL THE GAME--BUT *BIRD* WAS THE BETTER ALL-AROUND *PLAYER*.

!#$%@ *LARRY!*

"SHOWDOWN '84" WAS HIS BEST CHANCE TO PROVE THE PRO-BIRD CAMP WRONG.

THE SERIES DID NOT *DISAPPOINT*. THE TWO TEAMS *TRADED WINS* UNTIL RETURNING TO BOSTON GARDEN FOR GAME 7. IT WOULD BE THE HIGHEST-RATED GAME IN NBA HISTORY.

THE *UN-AIR-CONDITIONED* ARENA WAS A BRUTAL *91 DEGREES*.

THE CELTICS' *CEDRIC MAXWELL* LED THE ATTACK WITH 24 POINTS, 8 REBOUNDS, AND 8 ASSISTS.

STILL, THE LAKERS MANAGED TO CUT BOSTON'S LEAD TO A THREE-POINT DEFICIT WITH A MINUTE TO GO--MAGIC JOHNSON WAS POISED TO DO SOMETHING *DRAMATIC*--

--UNTIL MAXWELL KNOCKED THE BALL OUT OF HIS HAND.

THE PREDICTION THAT THE *FINESSE-HEAVY* LAKERS WOULD BE UNDONE BY THE TOUGHER, MORE *BRUTAL* CELTICS HAD COME TO PASS.

JOHNSON STAYED IN THE VISITORS' LOCKER ROOM FOR A HALF-HOUR AFTERWARD--CRYING.

A VICTORIOUS CELTIC CROWD ATTACKED THE LAKERS' BUS AS IT TRIED TO GET THE DEFEATED TEAM TO THE AIRPORT.

THE MEDIA LAID THE LAKERS' DEFEAT AT JOHNSON'S FEET--*"TRAGIC MAGIC"* HE WAS CALLED.

"IT WAS THE FIRST TIME IN MY LIFE I WAS *DEPRESSED*," HE CONFESSED.

THE LOSS STUNG COACH RILEY DEEPLY, AND HE ENTERED THE 1984-85 SEASON WITH HIS ALREADY-IRON RESERVE REDOUBLING. HE EVEN EXTENDED HIS SPEECHES TO THE *PLAYERS' WIVES:*

JUST SUPPORT OUR PLIGHT, AND YOU'LL WIND UP WITH BIG BUCKS AND A REALLY PRETTY RING.

WELL, YOUR HUSBAND WILL GET THE *REALLY* PRETTY RING. BUT WE'LL LET YOU RIDE ON A FLOAT IN THE PARADE.

PROBABLY.

NEVERTHELESS, THE CELTICS HUMILIATED RILEY'S LAKERS DURING THE REGULAR SEASON IN A 148-114 DRUBBING DUBBED *"THE MEMORIAL DAY MASSACRE."*

FEW OBSERVERS BELIEVED THE 1985 FINALS REMATCH BETWEEN THE TWO TEAMS WOULD TURN OUT MUCH DIFFERENT THAN THE PREVIOUS YEAR'S.

THIS WOULD BE THE *NINTH* TIME THE LAKERS FACED THE CELTICS--WITH BOSTON VICTORIOUS *ALL* THE PREVIOUS TIMES.

BUT ABDUL-JABBAR SCORED 29 POINTS AND TOOK THE MVP HONORS, WHILE JOHNSON WENT FOR A TRIPLE-DOUBLE (14 POINTS, 14 ASSISTS, 10 REBOUNDS) AS LOS ANGELES PREVAILED IN SIX GAMES-- THE FINAL VICTORY ALL THE *SWEETER* FOR TAKING PLACE IN *BOSTON GARDEN*.

THAT SUMMER, CONVERSE ASKED THE BIRD AND JOHNSON TO COSTAR IN A SNEAKER COMMERCIAL.

BIRD INSISTED MAGIC COME TO *FRENCH LICK* TO SHOOT IT. HE WAS LESS THAN THRILLED.

AND I THOUGHT *LANSING* WAS SMALL!

BIRD HAD BUILT A HOUSE FOR HIS MOM IN FRENCH LICK, COMPLETE WITH BASKETBALL COURT.

THE SCRIPT CALLED FOR THE TWO SUPERSTARS TO PLAY *ONE-ON-ONE* WITH EACH OTHER. THEY HAD TO FORCE THEMSELVES TO NOT TRY AND ONE-UP THE OTHER WHILE THE CAMERAS WERE ROLLING.

IN BETWEEN SHOTS, THEY SPENT REAL *TIME* WITH EACH OTHER FOR THE *FIRST* TIME.

MAGIC WAS GOING TO GO EAT IN HIS TRAILER, BUT LARRY INVITED HIM INTO THE HOUSE TO SHARE A LUNCH COOKED BY HIS MOM.

PREDICTABLY, THE BIRD FAMILY *ADORED* MAGIC--AFTER ALL, EVERYONE *ELSE* DID.

THAT PLEASANT DAY DID NOT DAMPEN THEIR **COMPETITIVENESS** IN-SEASON.

BIRD LED HIS CELTICS TO THE *1986* NBA CHAMPIONSHIPS, AND HE'D BE NAMED *FINALS MVP* FOR THE SECOND TIME AFTER LEADING THE DEFEAT OF THE HOUSTON ROCKETS.

WHEN BIRD'S CELTICS VANQUISHED THE UP-AND-COMING *DETROIT PISTONS* IN THE FOLLOWING YEAR'S PLAYOFFS, *DENNIS RODMAN* DENOUNCED BIRD AS "OVERRATED" BECAUSE OF HIS COLOR. HIS TEAMMATE *ISIAH THOMAS* AGREED:

I THINK LARRY'S A VERY, VERY GOOD BASKET-BALL PLAYER...I THINK HE'S AN EXCEPTIONAL TALENT...

BUT I'D HAVE TO AGREE WITH RODMAN. IF HE WAS BLACK, HE'D BE JUST ANOTHER GOOD GUY.

THOMAS WOULD CALL BIRD TO APOLOGIZE, SAYING HE MEANT IT AS A JOKE, BUT BIRD REFUSED TO LISTEN TO HIM, BECAUSE THAT WOULD IMPLY HE TOOK THE COMMENTS *SERIOUSLY* IN THE FIRST PLACE.

IF WHAT WAS SAID DOESN'T BOTHER ME, I DON'T THINK IT SHOULD BOTHER ANY OF US.

THE CELTICS WOULD ONCE AGAIN FACE LA IN THE 1987 FINALS, BUT WERE DISTRACTED BY LARRY HAVING TO HAVE A PRESS CONFERENCE TO PUBLICLY *RECONCILE* WITH THOMAS.

THE LAKERS WON THE SERIES IN *SIX*, FOREVER DISPELLING THE SPELL BOSTON HAD OVER THEM.

THEN MAGIC'S TEAM BEAT THOMAS'S PISTONS THE FOLLOWING YEAR TO BECOME THE FIRST NBA *BACK-TO-BACK CHAMPIONS* IN *TWENTY* YEARS.

MUCH OF THE NBA IN THE '80S WAS THE STORY OF *"MAGIC VERSUS THE BIRD,"* ONE WINNING CHAMPIONSHIPS, ONE WINNING MVPS, AND THE FANS OF EACH ARGUING THE OTHER WAS BETTER.

WHEN THAT CHANGED, IT CHANGED *QUICKLY*, AS IS SO OFTEN THE CASE IN SPORTS, BECAUSE OF *HEALTH*.

LARRY'S TROUBLES BEGAN WHEN HE INJURED HIS BACK SHOVELING GRAVEL TO MAKE HIS MOTHER'S DRIVEWAY.

HIS GRUELING STYLE OF PLAY TOOK A TOLL, AND HE LOST *STABILITY* IN HIS SPINE, MAKING HIS VERTEBRAE *LOCK UP* TO CREATE *ARTIFICIAL* STABILITY.

IN THE LAST FEW YEARS OF BIRD'S CAREER "BASKETBALL" BECAME SYNONYMOUS WITH *AGONY*. DURING IN-GAME BREAKS HE COULDN'T SIT ON THE BENCH. HE'D STRETCH OUT ON THE FLOOR TO TRY AND MANAGE HIS BACK PAIN.

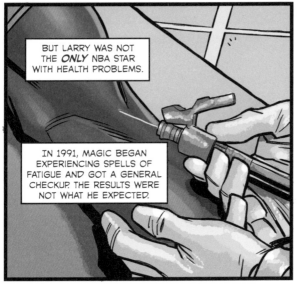

BUT LARRY WAS NOT THE *ONLY* NBA STAR WITH HEALTH PROBLEMS.

IN 1991, MAGIC BEGAN EXPERIENCING SPELLS OF FATIGUE AND GOT A GENERAL CHECKUP. THE RESULTS WERE NOT WHAT HE EXPECTED.

THE LAKERS TEAM PHYSICIAN TOLD HIM THAT HIS PHYSICAL HAD UNCOVERED THAT HE HAD TESTED POSITIVE FOR *HUMAN IMMUNODEFICIENCY VIRUS (HIV)*, THE VIRUS THAT CAUSES *AIDS*.

HOW IS IT POSSIBLE?

WHAT HAPPENED?

HOW DID IT HAPPEN TO ME?

HE HAD JUST GOTTEN *MARRIED* TWO MONTHS EARLIER--AND WAS EXPECTING HIS FIRST CHILD.

THE AIDS EPIDEMIC WAS ONE OF THE *GREATEST TERRORS* OF ITS AGE. THE DISEASE DEVASTATED THE IMMUNE SYSTEMS OF MILLIONS OF AMERICANS, DISPROPORTIONATELY GAY AND BISEXUAL MEN, BLACKS, AND LATINOS.

BY 1994, IT WOULD BECOME THE *LEADING CAUSE OF DEATH* AMONG TWENTY-FIVE- TO FORTY-FOUR-YEAR-OLDS WORLDWIDE.

MAGIC BEGAN TELLING PEOPLE PRIVATELY, AT FIRST. FORTUNATELY, NEITHER HIS WIFE NOR CHILD TESTED POSITIVE FOR THE VIRUS.

WHEN LARRY BIRD HEARD OF THE DIAGNOSIS THROUGH THE GRAPEVINE, HE WAS PRETTY SHOOK UP. HE CALLED MAGIC, WHICH GREATLY MOVED HIS LONG-TIME NEMESIS.

"YOU FIND OUT WHO YOUR FRIENDS REALLY ARE," MAGIC WOULD SAY LATER. "THAT WAS THE *GREATEST* MOMENT FOR ME, TO HAVE [LARRY] CHECK ON ME AND TO MAKE SURE I WAS OKAY."

ON NOVEMBER 7, 1991, MAGIC HELD A *PRESS CONFERENCE*:

BECAUSE OF THE HIV VIRUS THAT I HAVE ATTAINED, I WILL HAVE TO *RETIRE* FROM THE LAKERS TODAY.

IT WAS THE ONLY CONFERENCE IN WHICH SO MANY REPORTERS SAW EACH OTHER *CRY*.

FORMER TEAMMATES REFUSED TO PLAY WITH MAGIC OUT OF AN IRRATIONAL FEAR OF BECOMING SICK.

A CHARITY *ONE-ON-ONE* WITH FELLOW SUPERSTAR MICHAEL JORDAN WAS CANCELLED.

THE PUBLIC EXPECTED HIM TO WITHER AWAY AND *DIE* LIKE SO MANY OTHERS HAD IN THE DECADE BEFORE.

THE LIGHTS ON THE "SHOWTIME" ERA HAD GROWN *DIM*.

EVEN THE TACITURN *LARRY BIRD* PUBLICLY ADMITTED HOW MUCH THE NEWS SHOOK HIM.

THE ONLY TIME HE REMEMBERED FEELING LIKE THIS WAS WHEN HIS DIVORCED FATHER, BEHIND ON CHILD SUPPORT, SHOT HIMSELF IN HIS HEAD WITH HIS SHOTGUN.

THE BIRD NO LONGER HAD MAGIC TO MEASURE HIMSELF *AGAINST*. COMBINED WITH THE BACK PROBLEMS, LARRY'S CAREER RAPIDLY *DECLINED*.

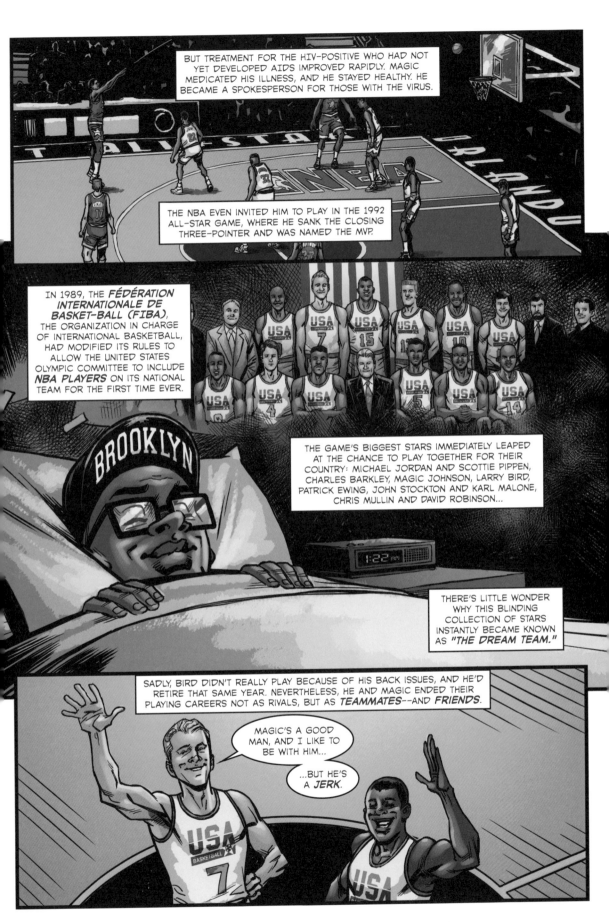

BUT TREATMENT FOR THE HIV-POSITIVE WHO HAD NOT YET DEVELOPED AIDS IMPROVED RAPIDLY. MAGIC MEDICATED HIS ILLNESS, AND HE STAYED HEALTHY. HE BECAME A SPOKESPERSON FOR THOSE WITH THE VIRUS.

THE NBA EVEN INVITED HIM TO PLAY IN THE 1992 ALL-STAR GAME, WHERE HE SANK THE CLOSING THREE-POINTER AND WAS NAMED THE MVP.

IN 1989, THE *FÉDÉRATION INTERNATIONALE DE BASKET-BALL (FIBA)*, THE ORGANIZATION IN CHARGE OF INTERNATIONAL BASKETBALL, HAD MODIFIED ITS RULES TO ALLOW THE UNITED STATES OLYMPIC COMMITTEE TO INCLUDE *NBA PLAYERS* ON ITS NATIONAL TEAM FOR THE FIRST TIME EVER.

THE GAME'S BIGGEST STARS IMMEDIATELY LEAPED AT THE CHANCE TO PLAY TOGETHER FOR THEIR COUNTRY: MICHAEL JORDAN AND SCOTTIE PIPPEN, CHARLES BARKLEY, MAGIC JOHNSON, LARRY BIRD, PATRICK EWING, JOHN STOCKTON AND KARL MALONE, CHRIS MULLIN AND DAVID ROBINSON...

THERE'S LITTLE WONDER WHY THIS BLINDING COLLECTION OF STARS INSTANTLY BECAME KNOWN AS *"THE DREAM TEAM."*

SADLY, BIRD DIDN'T REALLY PLAY BECAUSE OF HIS BACK ISSUES, AND HE'D RETIRE THAT SAME YEAR. NEVERTHELESS, HE AND MAGIC ENDED THEIR PLAYING CAREERS NOT AS RIVALS, BUT AS *TEAMMATES*--AND *FRIENDS*.

MAGIC'S A GOOD MAN, AND I LIKE TO BE WITH HIM...

...BUT HE'S A *JERK*.

CHAPTER EIGHT
G.O.A.T.

IN THE *DREAM*, THE MAN IS *PURSUED*:

"IT'S ALWAYS SOMETHING I'VE DONE.

"I HAVE ROBBED A BANK. OR I HAVE DONE COCAINE. I HAVE SUCCUMBED TO THE PRESSURES OF DRUGS. I HAVE FELT THE PRESSURE TO DRINK.

"THEY'RE NIGHTMARES OF SOMETHING TERRIBLE HAPPENING TO ME THAT WOULD DESTROY A LOT OF PEOPLE'S DREAMS OR CONCEPTIONS OF ME--THAT'S THE *BIGGEST NIGHTMARE* I LIVE EVERY DAY.

"WHAT IF I MADE A *MISTAKE*? THAT'S THE BIGGEST FEAR I FACE."

TO MANY, IT MAKES A PERVERSE SORT OF SENSE THAT *MICHAEL JORDAN* WOULD BE TORMENTED BY *DREAMS OF FAILURE.*

WHEW!

FROM THE OUTSIDE LOOKING IN, IT DID NOT APPEAR HE EXPERIENCED A WHOLE LOT OF FAILURE WHILE HE WAS *AWAKE.*

EVER SINCE HIS LEGENDARY 17-FOOT JUMP SHOT IN THE SUPERDOME WON THE NCAA CHAMPIONSHIP FOR THE NORTH CAROLINA TAR HEELS, JORDAN SEEMED DESTINED FOR A *CHARMED* BASKETBALL CAREER.

JORDAN EXCELLED AT *INNUMERABLE* ASPECTS OF THE GAME.

STAYING LOW TO THE FLOOR, KNEES BENT LIKE *COCKED PISTOLS*, HE WAS ABLE TO START AND STOP WITH INCREDIBLE SUDDENNESS.

HOW THE HECK DID HE *DO* THAT?!

HE COULD MAKE QUICK MICROADJUSTMENTS WITH THE BALL THAT OPPONENTS DIDN'T *SEE* UNTIL THEY *SLOWED IT DOWN* ON FILM.

JORDAN COMBINED THE FINESSE OF A *DR. J* WITH THE PHYSICAL POWER OF A *LARRY BIRD.*

HE EXCELLED AT VERTICAL *AND* HORIZONTAL JUMPING, CONTROLLING HIS BODY EQUALLY AS WELL *FIVE FEET OFF THE GROUND* AS ON THE HARDWOOD.

BUT IT WASN'T JUST THAT JORDAN **COULD** DO THESE THINGS--IT'S THAT HE DID THEM **CONSISTENTLY**, AGAIN AND **AGAIN**.

"MICHAEL JORDAN HAS THE **SENSATIONAL FLAIR** TO APPEAL TO THE MASSES," SAID PACERS COACH DICK VERSACE. "YET THE **PURIST** SEES THE UNSELFISHNESS, THE HIGH PERCENTAGE SHOTS THAT HE TAKES AND MAKES, THE GOOD CHOICES AND GOOD DECISIONS."

WHAT NEVER CHANGED IN ANY CIRCUMSTANCE, FRIENDS FROM NORTH CAROLINA SAID, WAS HIS WILL TO **WIN**:

"HE WAS THE MOST COMPETITIVE PERSON I'D EVER BEEN AROUND. PLAYING POOL, PLAYING PING-PONG, PLAYING VIDEO GAMES.

"HE'D PUT SWEAT INTO IT. HE'D BE PERSPIRING AND ARGUING EVERY POINT. HE MADE IT **FUN**."

HIS SUPERLATIVE **SKILL** WAS MATCHED BY A POSITIVE PERSONALITY THAT MADE PEOPLE **LIKE** HIM.

IT MEANT HE COULD BE A GREAT AMBASSADOR FOR THE GAME--AND **ANYTHING ELSE**.

BUT IN THOSE DAYS, IT WAS **UNHEARD OF** FOR COMPANIES TO GIVE PROMOTIONAL CONTRACTS TO **INDIVIDUAL** PLAYERS IN **TEAM** SPORTS.

THE NAME ON THE **FRONT** OF THE JERSEY WILL ALWAYS BE MORE IMPORTANT THAN THE NAME ON THE **BACK!**

SHOE COMPANIES AND **BASKETBALL** HAD BEEN INSEPARABLE FOR DECADES, STARTING WITH **CONVERSE**, MAKERS OF THE FIRST TRUE "SNEAKERS" IN THE 1960S, IMMORTALIZED IN A POPULAR 1981 AD:

CONVERSE ALL-STARS...**LIMOUSINES** FOR THE **FEET!**

NEVER HAD A SHOE BEEN MARKETED AROUND A **SINGLE PLAYER** BEFORE.

BUT THE **NIKE SHOE COMPANY** OF BEAVERTON, OREGON, WAS SLIPPING BEHIND COMPETITORS SUCH AS AEROBICS UPSTART **REEBOK** IN 1983. SUFFERING MASSIVE LOSSES, IT WAS WILLING TO TAKE A BIG RISK.

HERE'S THE DEAL, MJ--YOUR SIGNATURE MOVE IS THE **HORIZONTAL JUMP**, RIGHT?

SO I'D LIKE YOU TO MEET...THE **AIR JORDANS!**

"AIR JORDAN?" NOT THE "**MICHAEL JORDAN**"?

NAH. PEOPLE WILL THINK THEY'RE **DESIGNER JEANS**.

(THAT WAS THE ACTUAL REASONING.)

FUN FACT: THE NIKE LOGO WAS BASED ON A *LIFE* MAGAZINE PHOTO TAKEN OF JORDAN WHEN HE PLAYED IN THE 1984 OLYMPICS.

(TO GET A BETTER SHOT, THE PHOTOGRAPHER ENCOURAGED MJ TO DO A BALLET MOVE, THE GRAND *JETÉ*, INSTEAD OF HIS SIGNATURE JUMP!)

AFTER JORDAN SIGNED WITH THE *CHICAGO BULLS*, NIKE WOULD PAY HIM $2.5 MILLION A YEAR TO EXCLUSIVELY WEAR *AIR JORDANS*.

THERE WAS A *CLAUSE* IN JORDAN'S CONTRACT THAT SAID IF THE ROOKIE DIDN'T MAKE THE ALL-STAR TEAM *OR* ALL-NBA WITHIN THREE YEARS, NIKE COULD *DISCONTINUE* THE SHOE.

PROBLEM WAS--THE JORDAN DEAL HAPPENED SO *QUICKLY* THAT NIKE'S TEAM DIDN'T HAVE A CHANCE TO COME UP WITH A NEW DESIGN.

SO THEY TOOK A PRE-EXISTING BLACK-AND-RED SHOE AND JUST SAID:

MEET 〉HEH〈 THE AIR JORDAN!

THE CHICAGO BULLS WERE FURIOUS THAT THE SHOE DIDN'T MATCH THEIR OWN TEAM COLORS OF WHITE AND RED, SO THEY *FORBADE* JORDAN FROM WEARING THE SHOE...

...AND THEREBY HANDED NIKE *THE GREATEST MARKETING OPPORTUNITY* IN THE COMPANY'S HISTORY.

"ON OCTOBER 15, NIKE CREATED A *REVOLUTIONARY NEW BASKET-BALL SHOE.*

"ON OCTOBER 18, THE NBA THREW *THEM OUT OF THE GAME.*

"FORTUNATELY, THE NBA CAN'T KEEP *YOU* FROM WEARING THEM.

"AIR JORDANS. FROM NIKE."

(THEY WERE STILL UGLY.)

THE SOON-REDESIGNED SHOES WERE A MEGAHIT-- AND A MAJOR *STATUS* SYMBOL. THEY ACCOUNTED FOR *$130 MILLION* IN SALES IN THEIR FIRST YEAR.

HAD AIR JORDANS BEEN ITS OWN SHOE COMPANY, IT WOULD HAVE BEEN THE *FIFTH-LARGEST* IN THE *WORLD*.

SOON, JORDAN WAS APPEARING IN NIKE ADS DIRECTED BY (AND COSTARRING) UP-AND-COMING FILMMAKER *SPIKE LEE*.

DO YOU KNOW?
DO YOU KNOW?
DO YOU KNOW?

THE SUPERLATIVELY *SKILLED*, SQUEAKY-*CLEAN* JORDAN SINGLE-HANDEDLY DEMOLISHED CORPORATIONS' RESISTANCE TO USING *AFRICAN AMERICANS* AS PITCHMEN.

IN *COKE* ADS, HE WAS THE BOY NEXT DOOR--FOR *MCDONALD'S*, HE WAS THE BIG MAN ON CAMPUS--ON *CBS*, HE WAS A FRIENDLY BIG BROTHER.

HE WAS OFTEN COMPARED TO THE OTHER HUGE MAINSTREAM AFRICAN AMERICAN STAR-CUM-PITCHMAN OF THE '80S, *BILL COSBY*.

TO MAINTAIN HIS IMAGE, JORDAN WAS RELENTLESSLY-- SOME MIGHT EVEN SAY *MANIACALLY--APOLITICAL*. WHEN THE AFRICAN AMERICAN MAYOR OF CHARLOTTE, NORTH CAROLINA, *HARVEY GANTT*, RAN FOR THE U.S. SENATE SEAT OF NOTORIOUS SEGREGATIONIST JESSE HELMS, JORDAN REFUSED TO *ENDORSE* HIM, POINTING OUT:

"REPUBLICANS BUY SHOES TOO."

PERHAPS, AS IN HIS DREAM, THE INDOMITABLE JORDAN FEARED DISAPPOINTING *ANYONE* MORE THAN *ANYTHING*.

A NINTH-GRADE FAN OF JORDAN'S, MICHAEL EUGENE THOMAS OF MARYLAND, PAID *$115.50* FOR A PAIR OF AIR JORDANS IN 1989.

HIS GRANDMOTHER WARNED HIM NOT TO WEAR THE COVETED SNEAKERS TO SCHOOL. MICHAEL REPLIED:

GRANNY, BEFORE I LET ANYONE TAKE THOSE SHOES, THEY'LL HAVE TO *KILL ME*.

TWO WEEKS LATER, A SUPPOSED "FRIEND," DAVID MARTIN, AGE SEVENTEEN, STRANGLED MICHAEL THOMAS FOR HIS JORDANS AND LEFT HIS BAREFOOT CORPSE IN THE WOODS.

SCHOOL PRINCIPALS IN ATLANTA, DETROIT, NEW YORK, AND CHICAGO BANNED CERTAIN SHOE BRANDS FOR ENCOURAGING VIOLENCE--MUCH OF IT *DRUG-GANG* RELATED.

BY THE LATE '80S, *80 PERCENT* OF "BASKETBALL" FOOTWEAR WAS BEING BOUGHT AS A *FASHION STATEMENT*, NOT FOR COURT USE.

IF YOU DEAL DRUGS WE DON'T WANT YOUR MONEY, SPEND IT SOMEWHERE ELSE

SHOE COMPANIES TEST-MARKETED NEW STYLES IN THE INNER CITY, WHERE THOSE IN THE NARCOTICS TRADE COULD BEST AFFORD THEIR OVERPRICED PRODUCT. SOME SHOE *SELLERS* REBELLED.

WHEN TOLD OF THOMAS'S GRUESOME KILLING BY REPORTERS BEFORE A GAME, JORDAN CAME CLOSE TO TEARS.

I THOUGHT I'D BE *HELPING OUT* OTHERS AND EVERYTHING WOULD BE *POSITIVE*.

I THOUGHT PEOPLE WOULD TRY TO EMULATE THE *GOOD* THINGS I DO, THEY'D TRY TO BE BETTER.... EVERYONE LIKES TO BE *ADMIRED*, BUT WHEN IT COMES TO KIDS ACTUALLY *KILLING* EACH OTHER...

...THEN YOU HAVE TO *REEVALUATE* THINGS.

JORDAN'S *NIGHTMARE* OF DESTROYING PEOPLE'S *PERCEPTIONS* OF HIM SEEMED TO BE COMING *TRUE*.

HIS 1980S BULLS COULD NEVER GET PAST THE PESKY ISIAH THOMAS-LED "*BAD BOYS*" PISTONS IN THE PLAYOFFS.

HE BROKE HIS FOOT DURING THE 1985-86 SEASON, THEN REINJURED IT WHEN HE CAME BACK PREMATURELY.

THE PRESS COMPLAINED HE WAS OVERHYPED AND SELFISH.

FINALLY, THOUGH, IN A MORE-THAN-SYMBOLIC *CHANGING OF THE GUARD*, THE JORDAN BULLS DEFEATED THE LAST OF THE MAGIC *"SHOWTIME"* LAKERS TO TAKE THE 1991 NBA CROWN.

THERE WAS NO DOUBT WHO WOULD WIN THE FINALS *MVP* AWARD--ALONG WITH THE SEASON MVP.

THE FOLLOWING SEASON, THE BULLS PLAYED TO AN ASTOUNDING *67-15* REGULAR SEASON RECORD.

IN THE 1992 FINALS, JORDAN SCORED A RECORD 35 POINTS IN *THE FIRST HALF*.

AFTER SINKING HIS *SIXTH* 3-POINTER, SPORTSCASTER MARV ALBERT NOTED THAT JORDAN HIMSELF SEEMED TO BE SHRUGGING, SAYING, *"I CAN'T BELIEVE I'M DOING THIS."*

CHICAGO BEAT THE PORTLAND TRAIL BLAZERS IN *SIX*.

THE NEXT YEAR, JORDAN'S BULLS FACED HIS OLD FRIEND AND FORMER TEAMMATE (AND THAT YEAR'S MVP, ENDING HIS CONSECUTIVE STREAK) *CHARLES BARKLEY'S* PHOENIX SUNS AND BEAT *THEM* TOO.

JORDAN SCORED A RECORD 41 POINTS PER GAME AND WAS NAMED FINALS MVP FOR AN UNPRECEDENTED *THIRD YEAR IN A ROW*.

THEN, ALL OF A SUDDEN...

...HE CALLED IT *QUITS*.

I'VE ALWAYS STRESSED TO PEOPLE THAT WHEN I LOSE THE SENSE OF MOTIVATION, IT'S TIME FOR ME TO *MOVE ON*. I'VE REACHED THE *PINNACLE* AND I'VE ACHIEVED A LOT IN A SHORT PERIOD. I DON'T HAVE ANYTHING ELSE TO *PROVE*.

EVERYONE WANTS TO KNOW IF MY *FATHER'S DEATH* HAS ANYTHING TO DO WITH THIS.

PHIL JORDAN HAD BEEN MURDERED IN A CARJACKING THAT SUMMER IN NORTH CAROLINA. MICHAEL SAID:

"WELL, I WAS KIND OF *LEANING* IN THIS DIRECTION BEFORE, AND HE KNEW THIS. SO IT DIDN'T ALTER MY DECISION, BUT IN SOME WAYS IT MADE IT *SIMPLER*."

"WHAT MY FATHER'S DEATH MADE ME REALIZE IS HOW *SHORT* LIFE IS, AND HOW IT CAN BE TAKEN FROM YOU IN A *MINUTE*."

PHIL HAD BEEN A SEMIPRO *BASEBALL* PLAYER, AND IN A FAIRLY TRANSPARENT ACT OF OEDIPAL *FEALTY*, MICHAEL SIGNED A MINOR-LEAGUE CONTRACT WITH THE *CHICAGO WHITE SOX*, A TEAM ALSO OWNED BY THE BULLS' JERRY REINSDORF.

IN HIS 1994 DOUBLE-A SEASON WITH THE BIRMINGHAM BARONS, JORDAN BATTED AN ANEMIC .202 WITH 3 HOME RUNS AND 51 RBIS.

IT'S HARD TO SAY WHETHER OR NOT THE FAMOUSLY *TENACIOUS* JORDAN WOULD HAVE STUCK WITH BASEBALL HAD IT NOT BEEN FOR THE *1994–95 MLB PLAYERS' STRIKE*.

BUT ON MARCH 18, 1995, HE SENT OUT A TWO-WORD PRESS RELEASE:

"I'm back."

THE RUMORS THAT THE *REAL* REASON JORDAN WAS INSPIRED TO RETURN TO BASKETBALL AFTER PLAYING A GAME AGAINST ALIEN MONSTERS ON A TEAM WITH THE LOONEY TUNES AND BILL MURRAY APPEAR TO BE *UNFOUNDED*...

...BUT IT *IS* THE PLOT OF *SPACE JAM* (1996), THE LIVE-ACTION/ANIMATION MASH-UP THAT BOTH *PARODIED* AND MADE *EXPERT USE* OF JORDAN'S COMMERCIAL SKILLS, WHICH REMAINS, AS OF THIS WRITING, THE *HIGHEST-GROSSING BASKETBALL MOVIE OF ALL TIME*.

OTHER PLAYERS BEGAN TO FOLLOW THE JORDAN MODEL OF *PAN-MEDIA STARDOM*-- OR AT LEAST THEY *TRIED*.

SHAQUILLE O'NEAL, 7'1" AND 330 POUNDS, ROSE TO PROMINENCE DURING MICHAEL JORDAN'S DETOUR INTO BASEBALL.

HIS PENCHANT FOR TEARING DOWN HOOPS AFTER HIS DUNKS CAUSED SO MANY KIDS TO TRY *BENDING THE RIM* THAT PLAYGROUND MANAGERS COMPLAINED EN MASSE.

ACH!

THE AMIABLE, WITTY GIANT WAS NOT THE KAIJU-ESQUE MONSTER THE MEDIA MADE HIM OUT TO BE, BUT *"SHAQ ATTACK"* WAS A GREAT MARKETING HOOK.

SHAQ ATTACK!

PEPSI

SHAQ 33

I'M TIRED OF HEARING ABOUT MONEY, MONEY, MONEY, *MONEY*.

I JUST WANT TO PLAY THE GAME, DRINK PEPSI, WEAR REEBOK.

SHAQ WOULD BE NAMED ROOKIE OF THE YEAR IN 1993, TAKE THE ORLANDO MAGIC TO THE 1995 NBA FINALS IN JORDAN'S ABSENCE, AND WIN *FOUR* NBA RINGS...

...BUT BECAME AS WELL-KNOWN FOR BIZARRE MOVIES SUCH AS THE SUPERMAN-MYTHOS ENTRY *STEEL* AND THE KIDS' GENIE FLICK *KAZAAM*, WHICH MAKES *SPACE JAM* LOOK LIKE *CITIZEN KANE*.

THE **SECOND** CHAPTER OF JORDAN'S NBA CAREER WAS SOMEHOW EVEN MORE SPECTACULAR THAN THE **FIRST**.

ASSISTED BY BRILLIANT, ECCENTRIC POWER FORWARD **DENNIS RODMAN**, HIS BULLS DEFEATED THE SEATTLE SUPERSONICS IN SIX GAMES AND HIS AIRNESS WAS AGAIN NAMED SERIES MVP.

FITTINGLY, THEY CLINCHED THE CHAMPIONSHIP ON **FATHER'S DAY**, 1996.

UNBELIEVABLY, IN GAME 5 OF THE 1997 FINALS AGAINST THE UTAH JAZZ, JORDAN PLAYED WITH A RAGING FEVER--BUT **STILL** SCORED 38 POINTS IN A WINNING EFFORT.

HIS GREAT TEAMMATE SCOTTIE PIPPEN HAD TO HELP HIM OFF THE FLOOR. "I ALMOST PLAYED MYSELF INTO **PASSING OUT** JUST TO WIN A **BASKETBALL GAME**," JORDAN WOULD REMEMBER.

CHICAGO WON GAME 6, TOO, AND JORDAN HAD A **FIFTH** MVP AWARD TO GO WITH HIS **FIFTH** RING.

DESPITE BEING A REMATCH OF LAST YEAR'S BULLS VS. JAZZ FINALS, GAME 6 OF THE 1998 CONTEST GARNERED THE HIGHEST RATING OF ANY NBA GAME EVER--**18.7**-- AND MARKED THE FIRST TIME THAT THE NBA FINALS HAD MORE VIEWERS THAN THAT YEAR'S MLB **WORLD SERIES**.*

* NY YANKEES VS. SD PADRES

THE **RESULT** WAS THE SAME AS WELL--CHICAGO WON THE CROWN IN **SIX**, AND JORDAN WON SERIES MVP.

AND AFTER THIS SECOND **"THREE-PEAT,"** GUESS WHAT JORDAN DID **AGAIN?**

WITH HIS BEST TEAMMATES PIPPEN AND RODMAN MOVING ON TO OTHER TEAMS AND THE CONTRACT OF HIS COACH, PHIL JACKSON, EXPIRING, JORDAN ONCE AGAIN ANNOUNCED HIS *RETIREMENT* ON JANUARY 13, 1999.

THE STATE OF THE *LEAGUE* NO DOUBT AFFECTED HIS DECISION. AT THE TIME, NO GAMES WERE BEING *PLAYED* BECAUSE THE OWNERS HAD LOCKED OUT THE PLAYERS OVER A *"MERE"* $2 BILLION CONTRACT DISPUTE.

I AM *99.9 PERCENT* SURE IT'LL *STICK* THIS TIME!

MUCH OF THE PUBLIC SIDED WITH COMMISSIONER STERN AND THE LEAGUE, HAVING LITTLE PATIENCE FOR NICKELED-AND-DIMED *MULTIMILLIONAIRES*-- PARTICULARLY GIVEN THE RISING PRICE OF *TICKETS*.

SURPRISING NO ONE, THE FINALS RATING DURING THAT SHORTENED SEASON (KNICKS VS. SPURS) SANK FROM 18.7 TO A DISMAL *11.3*.

MANY WONDERED IF THE *PRO GAME* COULD SURVIVE WITHOUT ITS BRIGHTEST STAR.

THE *"0.1 PERCENT"* CAME TO PASS, AND JORDAN RETURNED TO THE GAME AGAIN IN 2001, TO PLAY FOR THE TEAM HE CO-OWNED AND HELPED MANAGE, THE *WASHINGTON WIZARDS*. HE PLEDGED TO DONATE HIS ENTIRE SALARY TO THE VICTIMS OF THE SEPTEMBER 11 TERRORIST ATTACKS.

HIS THREE, INJURY-PLAGUED SEASONS WITH THE WIZARDS ENDED IN A "THREE-PEAT" OF HIS *RETIREMENT* IN 2003-- AND THIS ONE *STUCK*.

IN THE YEARS SINCE HIS (LATEST) DEPARTURE, JORDAN'S LEGEND HAS GROWN TO THE POINT WHERE IT ALMOST SEEMS *UNBELIEVABLE*. AS HE WAS ASKED DURING THE '92 SUMMER GAMES:

YOU ARE SO GOOD--ARE YOU A TERRESTRIAL?

NO, I LIVE IN CHICAGO.

DR. STUART HAMEROFF, THE DIRECTOR OF THE CENTER FOR CONSCIOUSNESS STUDIES IN TUCSON, ARIZONA, HAS A THEORY:

"I THINK THAT CONSCIOUSNESS IS A SERIES OF *DISCRETE EVENTS*, DISCRETE FRAMES....A MOVIE APPEARS *CONTINUOUS*, TOO, BUT IN FACT IT IS DISCRETE FRAMES, OCCURRING AT ABOUT 30 HZ (HERTZ, OR CYCLES PER SECOND)...

"WHEN YOU THINK ABOUT *THAT* AND THEN YOU HEAR MICHAEL JORDAN SAY THAT WHEN HE WAS PLAYING AT CERTAIN TIMES, IT WAS LIKE EVERYTHING WAS IN *SLOW MOTION*--

"--WHAT IS LIKELY HAPPENING IS HE IS HAVING *MORE CONSCIOUS MOMENTS PER SECOND* THAN THE DEFENSE.

"IF THE DEFENSE STAYS AT 40 HZ, AND MICHAEL JORDAN IS ABLE TO RAISE HIS CONSCIOUSNESS UP TO *80 HZ*, HE IS SEEING *TWICE* AS MUCH AS THE OTHER PLAYERS AND IS ABLE TO PROCESS THAT MUCH MORE."

THIS WOULD EXPLAIN MANY OPPONENTS' AWED COMPLAINTS--THAT THEY KNEW *WHEN* AND *HOW* JORDAN WAS ABLE TO SCORE--BUT WERE *STILL* UNABLE TO *STOP* HIM!

TALENTED PLAYERS HAVE COME AND GONE SINCE JORDAN LEFT THE GAME. A FAVORITE PASTIME AMONG FANS AND PUNDITS IS DEBATING WHETHER OR NOT SO-AND-SO IS *GREATER* THAN JORDAN.

SO LET'S TRY A *THOUGHT EXPERIMENT*, SHALL WE?

LET'S SAY, IN THE FUTURE, THERE COMES A PLAYER...

YOU ARE SO GOOD--ARE YOU A TERRESTRIAL?

NO, I AM FROM THE PLANET *ZLIGNAZ*.

...THAT MANAGES TO *TOP* ALL OF JORDAN'S STATISTICAL ACCOMPLISHMENTS.

HE IS *SIX*-TIME NBA MVP TO MJ'S FIVE; *SEVEN*-TIME NBA CHAMPION INSTEAD OF SIX, WITH SEVEN NBA FINALS MVP TO GO WITH IT.

ELEVEN-TIME ALL-NBA FIRST TEAM; *TEN*-TIME NBA ALL-DEFENSIVE FIRST TEAM; *FIFTEEN*-TIME NBA ALL-STAR...AND SO ON.

EVEN IF SUCH A PLAYER EVER *EXISTED* OR *COULD* EXIST, HE *STILL* WOULD NOT BE AS GREAT AS *JORDAN*.

WHY?

30.1ppg

30.6ppg

BECAUSE JORDAN MADE BASKETBALL INTO THE *INTERNATIONAL SENSATION* IT IS TODAY. HE IS THE RARE ATHLETE WHO *TRANSCENDED* HIS SPORT WHILE SIMULTANE-OUSLY *EMBODYING* IT.

HE SHOULDN'T BE COMPARED TO ANY OTHER *BASKETBALL* PLAYER, BUT TO OTHER SUPERLATIVE ATHLETES SUCH AS *BABE RUTH*, WHO SIMILARLY PUT BASEBALL ON THE MAP WITH HIS--DARE WE SAY--*JORDAN-ESQUE* EXPLOITS.

AT THE TURN OF THE TWENTY-FIRST CENTURY, ESPN SURVEYED PLAYERS, SPORTSWRITERS, AND OTHER EXPERTS TO NAME THE *GREATEST ATHLETE* OF THE TWENTIETH CENTURY.

JORDAN CAME OUT ON TOP, *AHEAD* OF RUTH AND FELLOW CULTURAL ICON *MUHAMMAD ALI*.

WHAT, IN THE END, WAS HIS SECRET? JORDAN HIMSELF HAS SAID:

GREATEST OF ALL TIME (GET IT?)

"I'VE *MISSED* MORE THAN NINE THOUSAND SHOTS IN MY CAREER.

"I'VE *LOST* ALMOST THREE HUNDRED GAMES.

"TWENTY-SIX TIMES, I'VE BEEN TRUSTED TO TAKE THE GAME-WINNING SHOT AND *MISSED*.

"I'VE *FAILED* OVER AND OVER AND OVER AGAIN IN MY LIFE.

"AND *THAT* IS WHY I *SUCCEED*."

CHAPTER NINE
HOOPS WORLD

THOUGH BASKETBALL WAS INVENTED IN THE *UNITED STATES* BY A *CANADIAN*, ITS POPULARITY AND REACH HAVE EXTENDED FAR BEYOND *NORTH AMERICA*.

MISSIONARIES FROM THE YMCA, ORIGINATORS OF THE GAME, BROUGHT BASKETBALL TO *CHINA* IN THE LATE NINETEENTH CENTURY.

CHINA OFFICIALLY DECLARED B-BALL A *NATIONAL PASTIME* IN 1935.

THAT YEAR, MAO ZEDONG'S COMMUNISTS, ER, *APPROPRIATED* ANY BASKETBALLS THEY COULD FIND FROM THE VILLAGES THEY PASSED ON THEIR *LONG MARCH* TO ESCAPE THE NATIONALISTS DURING THE CIVIL WAR.

THE RED ARMY HUNG BAMBOO BASKETS AROUND THE ARTIFICIAL CAVE DWELLINGS NEAR YAN'AN THAT SERVED AS THEIR BASE.

MAO WAS OBSESSED WITH IMPROVING CHINA'S STRENGTH-- *LITERALLY*. SPORT WAS A HUGE PART OF THAT.

HIS EVENTUAL MINISTER OF SPORT, **HE LONG**, ORGANIZED A "FIGHTING ARMY TEAM" AND SNUCK INTO NATIONALIST TERRITORY TO PUT ON EXHIBITION GAMES AND CLINICS, WINNING THE HEARTS AND MINDS OF LOCAL VILLAGERS.

SOMETIMES THEY HAD TO **SHOOT** THEIR WAY BACK HOME AFTER THE GAME!

AFTER THE COMMUNISTS WON AND ESTABLISHED THE **PEOPLE'S REPUBLIC OF CHINA (PRC)**, GYMNASIUMS AROUND THE PRC DISPLAYED ONE OF MAO'S FAVORITE APHORISMS:

PROMOTE PHYSICAL CULTURE AND SPORTS AND BUILD UP THE PEOPLE'S HEALTH

STILL, CHINA REPEATEDLY CAME UP **SHORT** IN INTERNATIONAL COMPETITION, MUCH TO THE FRUSTRATION OF HE LONG. HE DEMANDED THAT THE NATION ACHIEVE AS MUCH IN **"BIG BALL"** SPORTS, LIKE BASKETBALL, AS THEY DID IN "SMALL BALL" SPORTS, LIKE **PING-PONG**.

IF WE DON'T REACH THE HIGHEST LEVEL IN THE **THREE BIG BALLS,*** I WILL NEVER SHUT MY EYES, NOT EVEN IN DEATH!

〉SNICKER〈

*SOCCER, VOLLEYBALL, BASKETBALL

THE PEOPLE'S REPUBLIC BEGAN RECRUITING **TALL CHILDREN** SO THEY COULD COMPETE BETTER IN BASKETBALL.

PROMISING **GIRLS** WERE SENT TO A FORMER BRITISH SOCIAL CLUB IN SHANGHAI, WHERE THEY ABIDED BY SAN JINZHONG, THE "**THREE TOGETHERS**": **LIVING**, **EATING**, AND **TRAINING** FOR EIGHT TO TEN HOURS A DAY, ON OUTDOOR COURTS THAT WERE BLAZING HOT IN SUMMER AND FREEZING COLD IN WINTER.

THE GRUELING SCHEDULE RENDERED MANY PLAYERS TOO **TIRED** TO **EAT**. MANY **CRIED THROUGH PAIN** DURING PRACTICE. SOME DEVELOPED **ULCERS** AND COULDN'T LOOK AT A BASKETBALL COURT WITHOUT **VOMITING**.

LITTLE WONDER THEN, WHEN THE *CULTURAL REVOLUTION* SWEPT THROUGH CHINA IN THE LATE 1960S, THAT THE PLAYERS-TURNED-RED-GUARDS *OVERTHREW* THEIR COACHES, FORCING THEM INTO A BRUTAL *"REEDUCATION."*

SPY! TRAITOR! ENEMY OF THE PEOPLE!

ONE OF THE MOST FERVENT OF THE RED GUARD AT THE SHANGHAI SPORTS SCHOOL WAS UP-AND-COMING STAR *FANG FENGDI*, NICKNAMED *DA ("BIG") FANG*.

DA FANG AND HER TEAMMATES WOULD "BARNSTORM" IN RURAL VILLAGES AS THE FIGHTING ARMY TEAM ONCE DID. THE GOVERNMENT DISPATCHED THE PRETTY CAPTAIN TO GREET ARRIVING DIGNITARIES AT THE AIRPORT.

行李提取 Baggage Claim ← | 转机 Transfers →

UPON HER RETIREMENT, 6' 2" DA FANG WAS ENTERED INTO A DE FACTO *ARRANGED MARRIAGE* WITH THE 6' 7" CAPTAIN OF THE MEN'S BASKETBALL TEAM, YAO ZHIYUAN, THE NEXT STEP IN WHAT WAS ESSENTIALLY A *BALLER BREEDING PROGRAM*.

AS PLANNED, WHEN THEIR FIRST (AND ONLY) CHILD, *MING*, WAS BORN IN 1980, HE WEIGHED *5 KILOS (11 LBS)*, TWICE AS MUCH AS AN AVERAGE CHINESE BABY.

AFTER THE CULTURAL REVOLUTION FADED, SHE BECAME THE BEST CENTER OF HER GENERATION, AND ROSE TO *CAPTAIN* THE CHINESE NATIONAL WOMEN'S TEAM.

4'11"

BY THE TIME HE WAS *SEVEN*, MING WAS 4' 11"--AS TALL AS THE NATION'S LEADER, *DENG XIAOPING*.

TYPICALLY, AN ATHLETE AS ACCOMPLISHED AS MING'S MOTHER COULD HAVE EXPECTED A HIGH POSITION IN THE *SPORTS MINISTRY* ONCE HER PLAYING DAYS WERE OVER.

BUT DA FANG'S PAST RETURNED TO HAUNT HER. THOSE COACHES SHE HAD TORMENTED DURING HER RED GUARD DAYS HAD RESUMED POWER AND *BLOCKED* HER ADVANCEMENT.

SHE HAD TO BEG FOR SCRAPS IN THE MARKET IN ORDER TO HAVE ENOUGH TO FEED HER PRETERNATURALLY *LARGE*--AND *HUNGRY*--LITTLE BOY!

NEVERTHELESS, THE PRC MADE SURE MING BEGAN TRAINING FOR BASKETBALL AT AGE *EIGHT*.

AT FIRST, HIS SIZE ADVANTAGE DID NOT APPEAR TO OVERCOME HIS LACK OF *SKILL*.

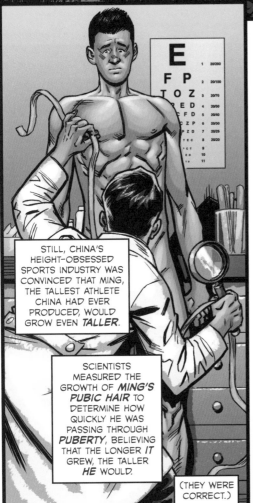

STILL, CHINA'S HEIGHT-OBSESSED SPORTS INDUSTRY WAS CONVINCED THAT MING, THE TALLEST ATHLETE CHINA HAD EVER PRODUCED, WOULD GROW EVEN *TALLER*.

SCIENTISTS MEASURED THE GROWTH OF *MING'S PUBIC HAIR* TO DETERMINE HOW QUICKLY HE WAS PASSING THROUGH *PUBERTY*, BELIEVING THAT THE LONGER *IT* GREW, THE TALLER *HE* WOULD.

(THEY WERE CORRECT.)

MING TOOK MEALS SEPARATELY FROM THE OTHER STUDENTS AT HIS ATHLETIC SCHOOL SO HE COULD EAT AS *MUCH* AS POSSIBLE.

HE WAS FORBIDDEN FROM *STRETCHING* WITH HIS TEAM FOR FEAR IT MIGHT SUPPRESS THE GROWTH OF HIS *LEGS*.

HE HAD TO BE MOVED TO A SINGLE ROOM WITH A SPECIAL 7' 10" BED TO ACCOMMODATE HIS UNUSUAL HEIGHT.

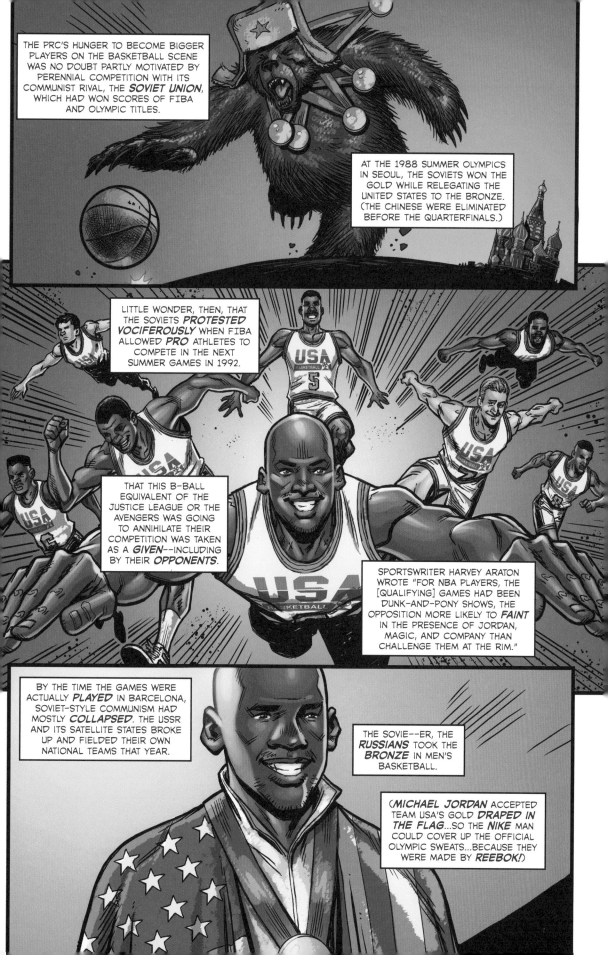

THE PRC'S HUNGER TO BECOME BIGGER PLAYERS ON THE BASKETBALL SCENE WAS NO DOUBT PARTLY MOTIVATED BY PERENNIAL COMPETITION WITH ITS COMMUNIST RIVAL, THE *SOVIET UNION*, WHICH HAD WON SCORES OF FIBA AND OLYMPIC TITLES.

AT THE 1988 SUMMER OLYMPICS IN SEOUL, THE SOVIETS WON THE GOLD WHILE RELEGATING THE UNITED STATES TO THE BRONZE. (THE CHINESE WERE ELIMINATED BEFORE THE QUARTERFINALS.)

LITTLE WONDER, THEN, THAT THE SOVIETS *PROTESTED VOCIFEROUSLY* WHEN FIBA ALLOWED *PRO* ATHLETES TO COMPETE IN THE NEXT SUMMER GAMES IN 1992.

THAT THIS B-BALL EQUIVALENT OF THE JUSTICE LEAGUE OR THE AVENGERS WAS GOING TO ANNIHILATE THEIR COMPETITION WAS TAKEN AS A *GIVEN*--INCLUDING BY THEIR *OPPONENTS*.

SPORTSWRITER HARVEY ARATON WROTE "FOR NBA PLAYERS, THE [QUALIFYING] GAMES HAD BEEN DUNK-AND-PONY SHOWS, THE OPPOSITION MORE LIKELY TO *FAINT* IN THE PRESENCE OF JORDAN, MAGIC, AND COMPANY THAN CHALLENGE THEM AT THE RIM."

BY THE TIME THE GAMES WERE ACTUALLY *PLAYED* IN BARCELONA, SOVIET-STYLE COMMUNISM HAD MOSTLY *COLLAPSED*. THE USSR AND ITS SATELLITE STATES BROKE UP AND FIELDED THEIR OWN NATIONAL TEAMS THAT YEAR.

THE SOVIE--ER, THE *RUSSIANS* TOOK THE *BRONZE* IN MEN'S BASKETBALL.

(*MICHAEL JORDAN* ACCEPTED TEAM USA'S GOLD *DRAPED IN THE FLAG*...SO THE *NIKE* MAN COULD COVER UP THE OFFICIAL OLYMPIC SWEATS...BECAUSE THEY WERE MADE BY *REEBOK!*)

EVEN THE **CROATIANS**, ON THE RECEIVING END OF THE DREAM TEAM'S GOLD MEDAL VICTORY--A **116-48 MASSACRE**--LOOKED DELIRIOUSLY HAPPY TO BE RECEIVING THE SILVER, AS IF THEY HAD ACTUALLY WON IT ALL.

THE FALL OF THE IRON CURTAIN ENCOURAGED A GREATER CULTURAL **OPENNESS**. OTHER COUNTRIES GOT TO WATCH THEIR COUNTRYMEN COMPETING AGAINST GREATS SUCH AS JORDAN--EVEN IF THEY GOT **SLAUGHTERED**--IMMEASURABLY **INCREASING** A LOVE OF HOOPS WORLDWIDE.

UNTIL THE YEAR BEFORE, CROATIA HAD BEEN PART OF THE COMMUNIST NATION OF **YUGOSLAVIA**, WHICH BROKE UP ALONG WITH THE USSR.

CALLING THE OLYMPIC RUN OF THE 1992 DREAM TEAM **THE SINGLE MOST IMPORTANT EVENT IN THE HISTORY OF GLOBAL BASKETBALL** IS NO HYPERBOLE.

CROATIA'S BEST PLAYER IN BARCELONA HAPPENED TO BE THE LEADING SCORER OF THE NEW JERSEY NETS, **DRAŽEN PETROVIĆ**.

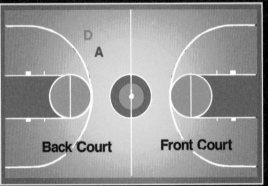

Back Court   Front Court

IN THE 1980S, DRAŽEN AND HIS BROTHER **ALEKSANDAR** WERE CONSIDERED THE BEST **BACKCOURT DUO** IN EUROPE, LEADING THE YUGOSLAV NATIONAL TEAM TO CHAMPION-SHIPS ON BOTH SIDES OF THE IRON CURTAIN.

YUGOSLAV LAW PROHIBITED PLAYERS FROM MOVING ABROAD UNTIL THEY TURNED **TWENTY-EIGHT**, BUT HIS SPANISH AGENT WAS TOLD TWO THINGS.

ONE: **EVERY** PROBLEM IN YUGOSLAVIA CAN BE SOLVED WITH THE RIGHT AMOUNT OF **MONEY**.

TWO: IF **DRAŽEN** LEAVES, EVERY **OTHER** PLAYER UNDER TWENTY-EIGHT WILL BE LEAVING AND IT WILL BE **CHAOS**.

SUFFICIENT **BRIBES** PERSUADED YUGOSLAVIA TO **PART** WITH THEIR BEST PLAYER AT THE TENDER AGE OF TWENTY-THREE.

PETROVIĆ SPENT JUST **ONE** SEASON WITH **REAL MADRID** BEFORE HE WAS TEMPTED TO TEST HIMSELF AGAINST THE NBA. THE PORTLAND **TRAIL BLAZERS** BOUGHT OUT HIS CONTRACT, BUT LARGELY KEPT HIM ON THE BENCH UNTIL TRADING HIM TO NEW JERSEY AT THE BEGINNING OF 1991.

OTHER FOREIGN-BORN PLAYERS, SUCH AS ZAIRE'S (NOW THE DEMOCRATIC REPUBLIC OF THE CONGO) **DIKEMBE MUTOMBO**, NIGERIA'S **HAKEEM OLAJUWON**, AND GERMANY'S **DETLEF SCHREMPF** HAD EXCELLED IN THE NBA, BUT THEY, LIKE THEIR AMERICAN COUNTERPARTS, HAD COME UP THROUGH THE NCAA COLLEGE SYSTEM.

PETROVIĆ WAS THE FIRST PLAYER TO COME FROM A FOREIGN **PRO LEAGUE** TO REALLY MAKE A NAME FOR HIMSELF IN THE NBA.

LIKE ALL **PIONEERS**, HE SUFFERED FROM THE IGNORANCE OF OTHERS--A KNICKS OPPONENT ACCUSED HIM DURING A GAME OF BEING INVOLVED WITH THE WORLD TRADE CENTER **TERRORIST ATTACK**.

(THERE ARE A LOT OF **PREJUDICES** AND **MISCONCEPTIONS** JUMBLED IN THAT ONE DIS: CONFUSING PETROVIĆ'S CROATIAN BACKGROUND WITH ITS MORE MUSLIM-DOMINATED EX-YUGOSLAV NEIGHBOR, **BOSNIA**; ASSUMING MUSLIMS ARE ALL TERRORISTS, ETC.)

DESPITE HAVING HIS BEST NBA SEASON FOLLOWING HIS OLYMPIC HEROICS AGAINST THE DREAM TEAM, PETROVIĆ FELT THE AMERICAN SYSTEM WAS **UNDERUTILIZING** HIM.

HE WAS SERIOUSLY CONSIDERING LEAVING THE NETS TO PLAY IN GREECE WHEN HE WENT TO BERLIN TO JOIN THE CROATIAN NATIONAL TEAM IN A QUALIFICATION TOURNAMENT FOR THE 1993 EUROBASKET.

ON JUNE 7, 1993, A TRUCK SWERVING TO AVOID A COLLISION ON A RAIN-SLICK HIGHWAY IN BAVARIA CRASHED THROUGH THE MEDIAN. A CAR IN WHICH PETROVIĆ WAS RIDING SLAMMED INTO THE TRUCK.

HE WAS NOT WEARING A SEATBELT, AND WAS KILLED INSTANTLY. HIS GIRLFRIEND, WHO WAS DRIVING, AND A FRIEND WERE SERIOUSLY INJURED.

HE WAS NOT QUITE **TWENTY-NINE YEARS OLD**.

IN DEATH, DRAŽEN PETROVIĆ ACHIEVED **MYTHIC STATUS**. MANY CONSIDER HIM TO BE THE GREATEST EUROPEAN PLAYER WHO EVER LIVED.

NOWHERE IS THIS TRUER THAN IN HIS NATIVE CROATIA. THAT YEAR, THE STADIUM FOR HIS FORMER PRO TEAM IN ZAGREB, KK CIBONA, WAS NAMED AFTER HIM. THE NETS RETIRED HIS JERSEY, AND HE WAS POSTHUMOUSLY INDUCTED INTO THE NAISMITH HALL OF FAME.

DRAŽEN PETROVIĆ

THIS EUROPE-TO-NBA PIPELINE WASN'T *ONE-WAY*, EITHER.

JOE *"JELLYBEAN"* *BRYANT* GRADUATED FROM PHILADELPHIA STREETBALL TO DR. J'S 76ERS.

THOUGH HIS NBA CAREER ENDED IN 1983 AT THE AGE OF TWENTY-NINE, BRYANT FELT HIS *BASKETBALL* CAREER DIDN'T HAVE TO BE OVER.

HE MOVED HIS FAMILY TO ITALY AND PLAYED FOR VARIOUS TEAMS IN THE *LEGA BASKET SERIE A (LBA)*, A PRO LEAGUE THERE SINCE 1920.

BRYANT'S WIFE, TWO DAUGHTERS, AND FIVE-YEAR-OLD SON WENT WITH HIM TO *RIETI*, IN THE CENTER OF THE COUNTRY.

INTERNATIONAL INFLUENCE WASN'T ENTIRELY *FOREIGN* (SORRY) TO THE FAMILY: THE BRYANTS NAMED THEIR SON *KOBE* AFTER THE FAMED BEEF FROM JAPAN.

KOBE GREW UP SPEAKING FLUENT *ITALIAN* AND HE COULD HEAR HOW MUCH THE LOCAL FANS ADORED HIS DAD.

("YOU KNOW THE PLAYER WHO'S BETTER THAN MAGIC OR JABBAR? IT'S JOSEPH, JOSEPH BRYANT!")*

* ITALIAN

KOBE HAD A VERY DIFFERENT BASKETBALL EDUCATION THAN WHAT THE SHOWY PLAYGROUND CULTURE OF INNER-CITY AMERICA HAD GIVEN HIS FATHER. HIS WAS *OLD-SCHOOL* IN A VERY *LITERAL* SINCE, HE'D LATER SAY:

"YOU KNOW, *BILL RUSSELL* AND *JERRY WEST*, THEY WERE GOING OVERSEAS AND DOING BASKETBALL CLINICS. SO THEY WERE TEACHING COACHES OVER THERE HOW TO *THINK* THE GAME, HOW TO PLAY FUNDAMENTALLY *SOUND*.

"I WAS A BY-PRODUCT OF ALL THAT. WHEN WE CAME TO PRACTICE, GUESS WHICH DRILLS WE WERE DOING? WE WERE DOING *RED AUERBACH'S* DRILLS--THINKING THE GAME *SEQUENTIALLY*.

"SO WHEN I CAME BACK TO AMERICA, ALL I HAD TO DO NOW WAS PUT THE ICING ON THE CAKE, IN TERMS OF THE *FLASH* AND THE *IMAGINATIVE* THINGS."

KOBE'S FATHER RETURNED THE FAMILY TO PHILLY AS KOBE ENTERED HIGH SCHOOL.

KOBE BECAME A HUGE HOOPS STAR WHILE STILL IN PUBLIC SCHOOL. TICKETS TO HIS GAMES WERE REGULARLY SCALPED, AND HE TOOK POP STAR *BRANDY* TO HIS SENIOR PROM.

BRYANT BUCKED NBA TRADITION BY SKIPPING COLLEGE AND GOING STRAIGHT TO THE PROS AFTER GRADUATION. HE BECAME THE FIRST GUARD EVER DRAFTED DIRECTLY OUT OF HIGH SCHOOL.

THE *CHARLOTTE HORNETS* HAD DRAFTED BRYANT, BUT THEN TRADED HIM TO THE LAKERS IN EXCHANGE FOR LA'S STAR CENTER. THE LAKERS USED THAT SAVINGS TO FREE *SALARY CAP SPACE* AND SIGN FREE-AGENT SUPERSTAR *SHAQUILLE O'NEAL*.

SHAQ AND KOBE BECAME "THE GREATEST ONE-TWO PUNCH EVER-- *LITTLE MAN, BIG MAN*-- IN THE HISTORY OF THE GAME," AS O'NEAL PUT IT.

MAYBE IT ACTUALLY *HELPED* THAT THE TWO *COULDN'T STAND EACH OTHER*.

O'NEAL EPITOMIZED THE BIG, BRASHY, "TOTALLY-IN-YOUR-FACE" STREET CULTURE THAT WAS ANATHEMA TO BRYANT'S O.G. TRAINING.

IT DROVE BRYANT *CRAZY* THAT SHAQ WOULD RELY SO MUCH ON HIS *PHYSICAL ADVANTAGES* TO DOMINATE THE RIM THAT HE (IN KOBE'S OPINION) DIDN'T EVEN BOTHER TO IMPROVE SOMETHING AS SIMPLE AS *FREE THROWS*.

THE BRYANT/O'NEAL LAKERS DIDN'T HAVE PLAYOFF SUCCESS UNTIL EX-BULLS COACH *PHIL "ZEN MASTER" JACKSON* WAS BROUGHT ON.

HE BALANCED THE ANTAGONISM OF HIS TWO STARS TO WIN A *THREE-PEAT* OF NBA CHAMPIONSHIPS FROM 1999 THROUGH 2001.

LAKERS OPPONENTS WOULD *"HACK-A-SHAQ"* TO *FOUL* O'NEAL, ROBBING HIM OF FIELD GOALS AND *FORCING* HIM TO THE FOUL LINE.

KOBE'S INTENSITY WAS TYPIFIED IN WHAT WAS CALLED HIS *"DEATH STARE."*

UPON WATCHING QUENTIN TARANTINO'S *KILL BILL*, HE STARTED TO CALL HIMSELF *"BLACK MAMBA"* AFTER UMA THURMAN'S CODE-NAME IN THE FILM.

THE SUB-SAHARAN SNAKE IS NOTORIOUS FOR ITS ABILITY TO STRIKE ACCURATELY AT MAXIMUM SPEED, IN RAPID SUCCESSION--LIKE KOBE ON THE COURT!

IF ANYTHING, "THE MAMBA" SUFFERED FROM BEING SO GOOD AT *EVERYTHING* THAT HE FELL BEHIND OTHERS IN *SPECIFIC* CATEGORIES.

ESPN RANKED HIM THE *SECOND* GREATEST SHOOTING GUARD BEHIND JORDAN. HE WAS AN ALL-STAR EIGHTEEN TIMES--*ONE* SHY OF ABDUL-JABBAR'S NINETEEN.

HIS FIVE NBA CHAMPIONSHIPS ARE TIED (WITH MAGIC) FOR MOST IN LAKERS' HISTORY-- THOUGH HE DID SURPASS ABDUL-JABBAR AS THE TEAM'S LEADING SCORER.

NEVERTHELESS, HE IS THE FIRST PLAYER WITH *30,000 CAREER POINTS* AND 6,000 CAREER *ASSISTS*.

WHILE KOBE AND SHAQ DOMINATED THE LEAGUE, *YAO MING* GREW TO ADULTHOOD UNDER THE CLOSE SUPERVISION OF CHINESE GOVERNMENT PHYSICIANS. HE WAS TOO TALL TO BE MEASURED BY STANDARD SCALES, SO HIS DOCTOR USED A BLUE PENCIL AGAINST A DOOR FRAME.

HIS HEIGHT CAREFULLY ENHANCED THROUGH HERBAL SUPPLEMENTS AND (IT WAS RUMORED) *HUMAN GROWTH HORMONE*, MING TOPPED OUT AT *7' 4"* WHEN HE WAS READY ENTER THE CHINESE PROFESSIONAL LEAGUE--THE TALLEST BASKETBALL PLAYER CHINA HAD EVER PRODUCED.

MING JOINED THE *SHANGHAI SHARKS*, THE BEST FRANCHISE IN A PRO LEAGUE CO-SPONSORED BY *NIKE*.

PLAN:

1. SPORT

2. ?????

3. PROFIT

BY 1994, A *THIRD* OF NIKE'S PRODUCTION HAD MOVED TO CHINA... BUT CHINESE PLAYERS STILL LARGELY WORE *CANVAS* SHOES.

NIKE'S MANTRA WAS "SELL THE *SPORT* FIRST, AND THE *PROFITS* WILL FOLLOW." CHINA'S INCREASING *URBANIZATION* ENCOURAGED BASKETBALL'S GROWTH.

THE *RED OXEN'S* (CHICAGO BULLS') *"SPACE FLIER"* (MICHAEL JORDAN) WAS VOTED ONE OF THE TWO MOST FAMOUS PEOPLE IN WORLD HISTORY BY CHINESE SCHOOLKIDS-- SECOND ONLY TO *MAO* HIMSELF.

BUT NIKE EXECUTIVES DESPAIRED OF EVER FINDING A CHINESE *STAR* FOR CHINESE *CONSUMERS* TO IDENTIFY WITH...

...UNTIL NIKE'S MAN IN CHINA WATCHED YAO MING SINK UNBLOCKABLE THREE-POINTERS FOR THE SHARKS.

BOYS, WE HAVE JUST SEEN THE *FUTURE* OF CHINESE BASKETBALL.

NEVERTHELESS, MING'S FAMILY WAS *SO POOR* THAT HE HAD TO WEAR *ADIDAS* SNEAKERS-- HAND-ME-DOWNS FROM A TEAMMATE OF DA FANG-- TO A *NIKE* PARTY!

NIKE ARRANGED TO HAVE A PAIR OF SIZE 18 AIR JORDANS SENT TO MING THE *VERY NEXT DAY!*

THE YEAR AFTER LEADING THE SHARKS TO THE CHINESE BASKETBALL ASSOCIATION (CBA) TITLE, MING TURNED *TWENTY-TWO* AND THE PRC COULDN'T STOP HIM FROM ENTERING THE NBA DRAFT.

HOUSTON, I AM COME!

BUT--TO SAVE FACE?--THE CBA ACTED LIKE THEY WOULD NOT LET MING PLAY IN THE STATES UNLESS HE WAS A *FIRST-ROUND PICK*--WHICH THE HOUSTON ROCKETS MADE SURE OF.

HE HAD TO PAY THE SHANGHAI SHARKS BETWEEN *8 MILLION AND 15 MILLION DOLLARS* TO GET OUT OF HIS CONTRACT, THOUGH.

开创大场面 和我们一起

NIKE GOT THE CHINESE STAR THEY WANTED. THE YEAR THAT YAO MING ENTERED THE DRAFT, 2002, THE COMPANY'S *INTERNATIONAL EARNINGS* OUTPACED ITS DOMESTIC PROFITS FOR THE FIRST TIME.

YAO WOULDN'T BE THE FIRST ASIAN PLAYER IN THE NBA--JAPANESE AMERICAN *WAT MISAKA* WAS A STAR FOR THE UNIVERSITY OF UTAH AND JOINED THE NEW YORK KNICKS IN *1947*.

THE SAME YEAR THAT JACKIE ROBINSON BROKE THE COLOR BARRIER IN MAJOR LEAGUE BASEBALL, MISAKA BECAME THE FIRST *NONWHITE PLAYER* IN THE BAA, THE NBA'S FORERUNNER.

THE QUESTION, THEN, WAS WHETHER OR NOT YAO COULD BECOME THE *CHINESE DRAŽEN PETROVIĆ*-- A PRO FROM A FOREIGN LEAGUE WHO HAD THE SKILLS TO MAKE IT IN THE NBA.

TNT COMMENTATOR *CHARLES BARKLEY* MOCKED THE ROCKETS FOR THE SIGNING AND SWORE HE'D KISS HIS CO-ANCHOR'S *ASS* IF THE CHINESE STAR SCORED NINETEEN POINTS IN ANY GAME THAT SEASON.

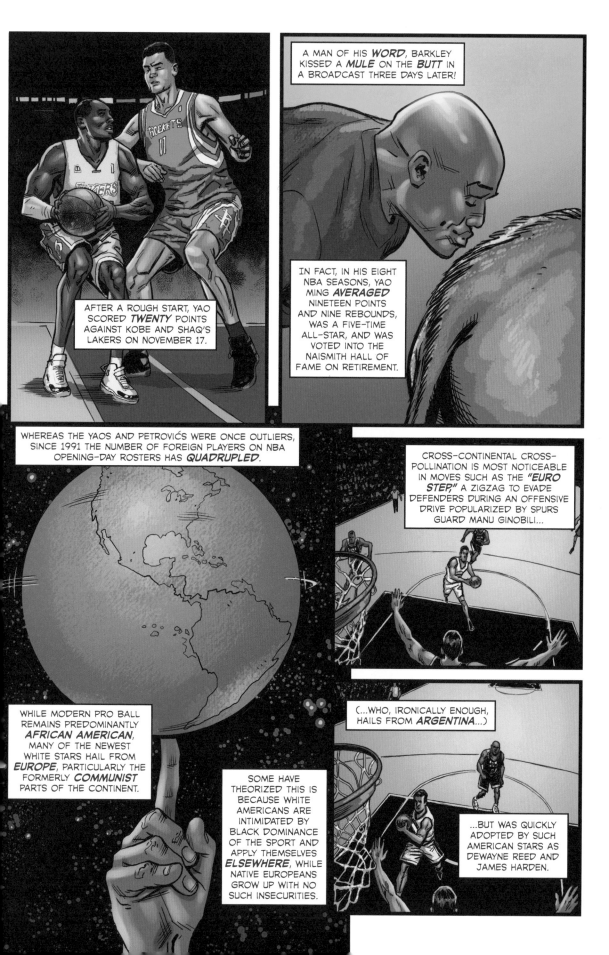

AFTER A ROUGH START, YAO SCORED *TWENTY* POINTS AGAINST KOBE AND SHAQ'S LAKERS ON NOVEMBER 17.

A MAN OF HIS *WORD*, BARKLEY KISSED A *MULE* ON THE *BUTT* IN A BROADCAST THREE DAYS LATER!

IN FACT, IN HIS EIGHT NBA SEASONS, YAO MING *AVERAGED* NINETEEN POINTS AND NINE REBOUNDS, WAS A FIVE-TIME ALL-STAR, AND WAS VOTED INTO THE NAISMITH HALL OF FAME ON RETIREMENT.

WHEREAS THE YAOS AND PETROVIĆS WERE ONCE OUTLIERS, SINCE 1991 THE NUMBER OF FOREIGN PLAYERS ON NBA OPENING-DAY ROSTERS HAS *QUADRUPLED*.

WHILE MODERN PRO BALL REMAINS PREDOMINANTLY *AFRICAN AMERICAN*, MANY OF THE NEWEST WHITE STARS HAIL FROM *EUROPE*, PARTICULARLY THE FORMERLY *COMMUNIST* PARTS OF THE CONTINENT.

SOME HAVE THEORIZED THIS IS BECAUSE WHITE AMERICANS ARE INTIMIDATED BY BLACK DOMINANCE OF THE SPORT AND APPLY THEMSELVES *ELSEWHERE*, WHILE NATIVE EUROPEANS GROW UP WITH NO SUCH INSECURITIES.

CROSS-CONTINENTAL CROSS-POLLINATION IS MOST NOTICEABLE IN MOVES SUCH AS THE *"EURO STEP,"* A ZIGZAG TO EVADE DEFENDERS DURING AN OFFENSIVE DRIVE POPULARIZED BY SPURS GUARD MANU GINOBILI...

(...WHO, IRONICALLY ENOUGH, HAILS FROM *ARGENTINA*...)

...BUT WAS QUICKLY ADOPTED BY SUCH AMERICAN STARS AS DEWAYNE REED AND JAMES HARDEN.

TODAY, THE NBA IS BROADCAST IN MORE THAN *215* COUNTRIES AND TERRITORIES. BY MANY METRICS, ITS BIGGEST MARKET IS *CHINA*, WHERE YAO MING HAS BEEN PRESIDENT OF THE CHINESE BASKETBALL ASSOCIATION SINCE FEBRUARY 2017--ACHIEVING THE HEIGHTS OF OFFICIALDOM HIS MOTHER WAS DENIED.

THE ONLY PLAYER CLOSE IN POPULARITY TO YAO IN HIS NATIVE LAND IS *KOBE BRYANT.*

BRYANT HOSTED BASKETBALL CLINICS IN CHINA STARTING IN 1998, JUST AS STARS SUCH AS BILL RUSSELL HAD DONE IN ITALY WHEN KOBE WAS GROWING UP.

IN 2008, HE STARRED IN A REALITY SHOW, *KOBE MENTU* (KOBE'S DISCIPLES), IN WHICH CHINESE PLAYERS TRAINED FOR TWO WEEKS UNDER BRYANT'S INTENSE WATCH.

THE FOLLOWING YEAR, HE CREATED THE *KOBE BRYANT CHINA FUND* AND DONATED FIVE MILLION YUAN ($700,000) TO SICHUAN PROVINCE, DEVASTATED BY AN EARTHQUAKE.

WHEN THE NBA SUFFERED YET ANOTHER LABOR STOPPAGE IN AUGUST 2011, RUMORS RIPPLED THROUGH CHINA THAT BRYANT WAS THINKING OF COMING TO PLAY FOR THE CBA'S SHANXI BRAVE DRAGONS.

BRYANT'S WORLD-WIDE PHILANTHROPY CONTINUED WELL AFTER HIS RETIRE-MENT, UNTIL HIS TRAGIC DEATH IN A HELICOPTER CRASH ON JANUARY 26, 2020, JUST AS THIS BOOK WAS BEING COMPLETED.

ARRIVING IN BEIJING TO PLAY WITH BRYANT IN THE 2008 SUMMER OLYMPICS, A STUNNED LEBRON JAMES DECLARED:

I THOUGHT *I* WAS FAMOUS...

...UNTIL I GOT HERE WITH *KOBE!*

SHANXI 24

CHAPTER TEN
DREAM TEAMS

WHEN TEN-YEAR-OLD *REBECCA LOBO* WROTE RED AUERBACH PREDICTING SHE'D BE THE FIRST FEMALE *CELTIC*, HER DREAM WAS NOT AS OUTLANDISH AS IT MIGHT FIRST SOUND.

THE FIRST GENERATION OF *TITLE IX-ERA* WOMEN'S BASKETBALL PLAYERS WERE GRADUATING FROM COLLEGE, AND THE PROS WERE *INTRIGUED*.

THE NEW ORLEANS JAZZ ACTUALLY SELECTED *LUISA HARRIS* OF THE AIAW-CHAMPION *DELTA STATE LADY STATESMEN* AS A SEVENTH-ROUND PICK IN 1977, MAKING HER THE FIRST WOMAN TO EVER *OFFICIALLY* BE DRAFTED INTO THE NBA.

HARRIS, HOWEVER, WASN'T PARTICULARLY *INTERESTED* IN PLAYING MEN'S BASKETBALL AND DECLINED TO SIGN...

...A DECISION PROBABLY MADE *EASIER* BY THE FACT SHE WAS *PREGNANT* AT THE TIME AND COULDN'T ATTEND TRYOUTS.

IN 1980, THE INDIANA PACERS SIGNED UCLA STAR *ANN MEYERS* TO A NO-CUT CONTRACT, BUT SHE FAILED TO MAKE THE TEAM.

A CHICAGO BUSINESSMAN NAMED **BILL BYRNE**, PRESIDENT OF THE NATIONAL SCOUTING ASSOCIATION, STARTED A **WOMEN'S PROFESSIONAL BASKETBALL LEAGUE (WBL)** WITH EIGHT FRANCHISES IN 1978.

ANN MEYERS WAS THE **FIRST PICK** IN THE FIRST WBL DRAFT BY THE **NEW JERSEY GEMS.**

THE **HOUSTON ANGELS** PICKED LUISA HARRIS.

BUT THE FIRST TO **SIGN** WITH THE WBL WAS HIGH SCHOOL STAR **MOLLY BOLIN**, WHO HAD BEEN DRAFTED BY HER HOME-STATE **IOWA CORNETS.**

BLONDE, BLUE-EYED, AND BEAUTIFUL, BOLIN QUICKLY BECAME THE **FEATURED PLAYER** IN THE LEAGUE'S MARKETING MATERIALS FOR ALL THE **OBVIOUS** (SEXIST) REASONS.

(THIS WAS THE ACTUAL PHOTO POSE FOR HER **SPORTS ILLUSTRATED** INTERVIEW.)

PEOPLE ALWAYS WARNED ME ABOUT **EXPLOITATION**, BUT IT'S ALL ABOUT PUTTING PEOPLE IN THE **SEATS**, ISN'T IT?

IF YOU REALLY WANT TO MAKE IT WHEN YOU'RE **NEW**, YOU'VE GOT TO GRAB EVERYTHING YOU **GOT** AND GO WITH IT.

WHAT BOLIN **HAD** WAS **GAME**. A SKILLED **TURNAROUND JUMPER** OFTEN COMPARED TO LARRY BIRD, **"MACHINE GUN MOLLY"** LED THE LEAGUE IN SCORING DURING HER ROOKIE YEAR.

SHE **STILL** HOLDS THE RECORD FOR THE MOST POINTS SCORED BY A PROFESSIONAL FEMALE PLAYER IN A SINGLE GAME (55) AND REGULAR SEASON SCORING AVERAGE (32.8).

WBL PLAYERS SIGNED FOR *PALTRY* SALARIES THAT OFTEN WENT *UNPAID.*

THE NEW ENGLAND GULLS HAD TO SNEAK INTO THE MERRIMACK COLLEGE CAFETERIA AND *STEAL FOOD* FOR BREAKFAST BECAUSE THEY COULDN'T AFFORD GROCERIES.

FED UP, THE GULLS PLAYERS *QUIT* EN MASSE ON THE DAY OF A SCHEDULED GAME.

CANCELED

NEW ENGLAND GULLS

THE TEAM'S OWNER HAD HIS LICENSE YANKED; APPARENTLY HE HAD A REPUTATION AROUND BOSTON AS A FLIMFLAM ARTIST.

ONE OF THE PLAYERS WAS APPROACHED BY A SHADY CHARACTER WHO ASKED IF THE OWNER SHOULD BE "TAKEN CARE OF."

I DON'T THINK WE'LL HAVE TO RESORT TO THAT...

PRO BBALL LEAGUES

A FEW NBA FRANCHISES, LIKE THE SAN FRANCISCO WARRIORS, OFFERED TO HELP OUT THEIR WBL COUNTERPARTS, BUT THE REMAINING OWNERS FAILED TO DRUM UP ENOUGH INVESTMENT TO SUPPORT THE LEAGUE. IT CEASED OPERATIONS ON SEPTEMBER 24, 1981.

WOMEN'S DIVISION

WPBL 1978 1981

AS WITH MEN'S PRO LEAGUES EARLIER IN THE CENTURY, A STREAM OF ENTREPRENEURS AND DREAMERS TRIED TO OPEN A *WOMEN'S* LEAGUE--AND FAILED.

TALENTED AMERICAN WOMEN KNEW THEY COULD MAKE MORE MONEY PLAYING IN THE *EUROPEAN* PRO LEAGUES AFTER COLLEGE.

EuroLeague

FIBA HAS RUN *EURO-LEAGUE WOMEN* SINCE *1958*, A DECADE AND A HALF BEFORE TITLE IX HAD EVEN PASSED.

COMMUNIST COUNTRIES, AS A WHOLE, WERE *WAY AHEAD* OF THEIR WESTERN COUNTERPARTS IN THEIR SUPPORT FOR WOMEN'S SPORTS, WHICH MAY EXPLAIN WHY EUROPE ADOPTED PRO WOMEN'S TEAMS MUCH EARLIER.

THE FIRST DOMINANT TEAM OF EUROLEAGUE WOMEN WAS *DAUGAVA RIGA* FROM WHAT IS NOW LATVIA, BUT THEN PART OF THE *SOVIET UNION*.

RIGA WON *16 OUT OF 17 FINALS* BETWEEN 1960 AND 1977.

SUPERIOR *TRAINING* MET WITH SUPERIOR *RESULTS*. WHILE THE "DREAM TEAM" COMPRISING (FOR THE FIRST TIME) PROFESSIONAL *MALE* PLAYERS DEMOLISHED THE COMPETITION AT BARCELONA IN 1992...

...THE AMERICAN *WOMEN* WERE HUMILIATED BY A *THIRD-PLACE* FINISH BEHIND RUSSIA (GOLD) AND THE PEOPLE'S REPUBLIC OF CHINA (SILVER).

THE *1996* SUMMER OLYMPICS WERE GOING TO BE HELD IN THE UNITED STATES--IN ATLANTA, GEORGIA--AND USA BASKETBALL WAS DETERMINED TO NOT SETTLE FOR ANYTHING LESS THAN *GOLD* THIS TIME.

THE WOMEN'S PROGRAM BEGAN ASSEMBLING A *"DREAM TEAM"* OF ITS OWN.

THOUGH THIRTY-TWO YEARS OLD, *TERESA EDWARDS* WAS STILL CONSIDERED THE BEST WOMEN'S PLAYER IN THE WORLD, SPENDING NINE YEARS AFTER GRADUATION FROM THE UNIVERSITY OF GEORGIA PLAYING IN ITALY, JAPAN, SPAIN, AND FRANCE.

HER TEAMMATE *SHERYL SWOOPES* WAS EQUALLY ACCOMPLISHED, SETTING NUMEROUS NCAA RECORDS FOR SINGLE-GAME SCORING (53) AND SINGLE-SEASON SCORING (955) WHILE AT TEXAS TECH.

SWOOPES PRACTICALLY BEAT OHIO STATE FOR THE NCAA CHAMPIONSHIP *HERSELF*, DESPITE THE BUCKEYES' COACH INVENTING A SPECIAL *2-3 ZONE DEFENSE* TO TRY AND CONTAIN HER!

LIKE EDWARDS, SHE TRIED THE PRO GAME IN ITALY. *HOMESICK*, SHE RETURNED TO THE US WITHIN THREE MONTHS.

SHE STAYED IN SHAPE AND BECAME THE FIRST FEMALE PLAYER TO HAVE HER OWN NIKE SHOE, THE AIR SWOOPES ($115/PAIR).

ALSO MAKING THE USA TEAM WAS *LISA LESLIE*, WHO HAD TAUGHT HERSELF TO SHOOT *AMBIDEXTROUSLY* SO SHE WOULDN'T HAVE TO BE THE ONLY LEFT-HANDED PLAYER ON HER TEAM.

WHILE PLAYING FOR THE UNIVERSITY OF SOUTHERN CALIFORNIA (USC), LESLIE SET PAC-10 *RECORDS* FOR SCORING, REBOUNDING, AND BLOCKING SHOTS.

THE YOUNGEST PLAYER ON THE TEAM WAS NONE OTHER THAN *REBECCA LOBO*, WHO HAD JUST LED HER UNIVERSITY OF CONNECTICUT (UCONN) HUSKIES TO A 35-0 RECORD AND THE NCAA CHAMPIONSHIP.

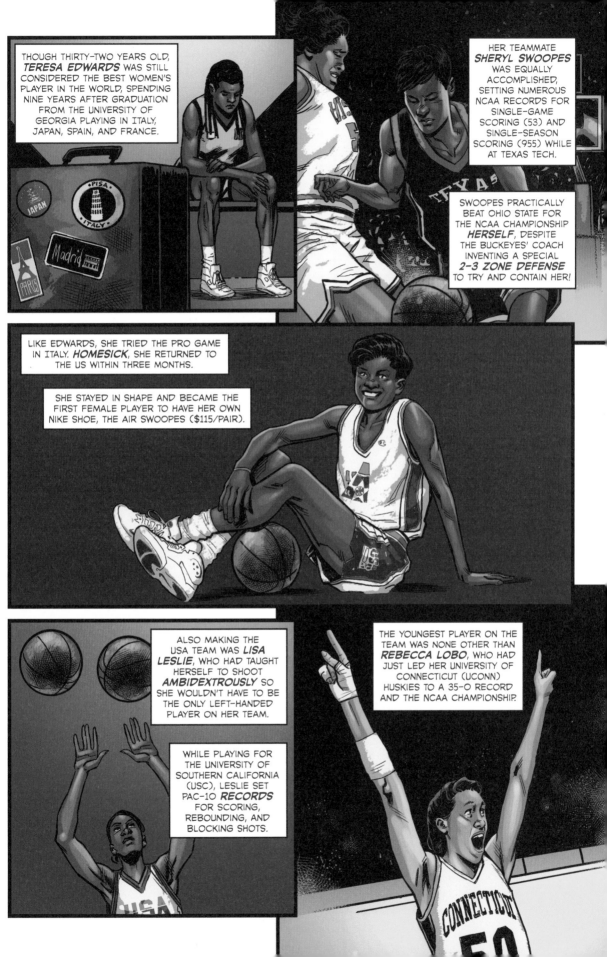

REAL BASKETBALL.

AS TEAM USA TRAINED FOR ATLANTA, A GROUP OF BUSINESSPEOPLE ANNOUNCED ANOTHER STAB AT A WOMEN'S PRO LEAGUE, THE **AMERICAN BASKET-BALL LEAGUE (ABL),** WHICH WOULD BEGIN PLAY IN OCTOBER 1996, NOT LONG AFTER THE AMERICAN WOMEN (HOPEFULLY) SECURED OLYMPIC GOLD.

THE WIND WAS TAKEN OUT OF THE ABL'S SAILS (AND SALES), HOWEVER, WHEN THE BIG BOY ON THE BLOCK, THE **NBA,** ANNOUNCED THEY WOULD START THEIR OWN WOMEN'S LEAGUE THE FOLLOWING YEAR.

WITH THE NBA'S STAMP OF APPROVAL, THE SWOOPES AND LESLIES OF THE WORLD BAILED ON THE SMALLER ABL.

TENSIONS WITHIN TEAM USA GREW AS PLAYERS SIDED WITH EITHER THE ABL OR THE NEW WOMEN'S NATIONAL BASKETBALL ASSOCIATION (WNBA).

"THIS ISN'T PERSONAL," SHERYL SWOOPES SAID. "I DON'T THINK PEOPLE SHOULD GET MAD WITH EACH OTHER. TO ME, WHAT THIS MEANS IS THERE IS A LOT OF INTEREST IN WOMEN'S BASKETBALL."

INDEED, AS TEAM USA STARTED PLAYING AROUND THE COUNTRY, THEY SAW MORE AND MORE LITTLE GIRLS IN THE STANDS, AND REALIZED HOW *INSPIRING* AN ALL-WOMEN'S LEAGUE COULD BE.

THE IDEA OF A **WOMEN'S** PRO LEAGUE ALSO BENEFITED FROM A SPIKE IN CYNICISM ABOUT **MEN'S** SPORTS. THE MLB STRIKE OF 1994 HAD CANCELLED THE WORLD SERIES AND NEARLY RUINED THE SPORT.

ESPN COMMENTATOR ROBIN ROBERTS SAID, "THE WOMEN IN BASKETBALL ARE PLAYING FOR THE **SHEER JOY** AND LOVE OF THE GAME, SOMETHING THE PUBLIC RECOGNIZES."

GEORGIA-NATIVE **TERESA EDWARDS** WAS CHOSEN TO MAKE THE **ATHLETES' OATH** DURING THE OPENING CEREMONIES ON JULY 19, 1996--**HER BIRTHDAY.**

TEAM USA CRUISED TO THE FIRST MEDAL ROUND BY ROUNDLY DEFEATING CUBA, UKRAINE, AND ZAIRE.

THE DAY THEY WERE SCHEDULED TO FACE AUSTRALIA, MANY PLAYERS WERE AWAKENED BY THE SOUND OF AN EXPLOSION IN **CENTENNIAL OLYMPIC PARK** BELOW.

BWHOOM

A RIGHT-WING TERRORIST HAD HOPED TO CANCEL THE OLYMPICS BY DETONATING PIPE BOMBS THAT THREW OUT MASONRY NAILS, INJURING 111 PEOPLE AND KILLING A SINGLE PERSON DIRECTLY.

THE COWARDLY ATTACK FAILED IN ITS INTENDED PURPOSE, HOWEVER--**33,000 FANS** PACKED THE STADIUM THAT NIGHT TO WATCH TEAM USA DEFEAT TEAM AUSTRALIA, 96-79.

LISA LESLIE SET A US OLYMPIC RECORD WITH 35 POINTS AGAINST JAPAN IN THE QUARTERFINALS.

THEY FACED AUSTRALIA IN A REMATCH FOR THE SEMIFINALS, BUT OUTWITTED THEIR OPPONENTS BY SWITCHING FROM MAN-TO-MAN TO **ZONE** DEFENSE.

THE COACH, STANFORD'S TARA VANDERVEER, HAD COMPILED A VIDEOTAPE OF AMERICAN WOMEN WINNING **GOLD MEDALS** AND SHOWED IT TO HER PLAYERS THE NIGHT BEFORE THE GAME.

IT HAD BEEN **TWENTY-FOUR YEARS** SINCE TITLE IX PASSED, AND THE PLAYERS UNDERSTOOD THAT THEY WERE THE FIRST OF A **NEW GENERATION** OF AMERICAN ATHLETES--WOMEN WHO HAD THE SAME GUARANTEES UNDER THE LAW TO ACHIEVE AT SPORT IN THE SAME WAY THEIR MALE COUNTERPARTS DID.

VANDERVEER'S INSPIRATION *WORKED*. TEAM USA *WALLOPED* UNDEFEATED BRAZIL IN A 25-POINT ROUT TO TAKE THE GOLD.

AMERICAN WOMEN SANK 72 PERCENT OF THEIR SHOTS AND SCORED IN 11 OUT OF 12 POSSESSIONS IN THE SECOND HALF.

THE AMERICAN BASKETBALL LEAGUE, RIDING THE OLYMPIC VICTORY WAVE, OPENED ITS FIRST SEASON ON OCTOBER 18, 1996, BEFORE 8,767 SPECTATORS IN THE HOME OF REBECCA LOBO'S HUSKIES-- HARTFORD, CONNECTICUT.

THE POPULARITY OF THE ABL EVEN TOOK THE *LEAGUE* BY SURPRISE--THEY AVERAGED 3,500 FANS PER GAME, 20 PERCENT *HIGHER* THAN THEIR INITIAL PROJECTIONS. BY ITS SECOND YEAR, SEASON TICKET SALES WERE UP *30 PERCENT!*

BUT THE ABL WAS *DOOMED* FROM THE START BECAUSE ITS REGIONAL MARKETS WERE TOO SMALL TO ATTRACT MAJOR *TV CONTRACTS*. AND THE BIG, BAD BULLY OF THE (W)NBA LURKED IN THE WINGS.

MOST OF 1996'S OLYMPIC HEROES CHOSE TO SIGN WITH THE WNBA.

THE FIRST WNBA GAME DEBUTED (ON *TELEVISION*, NO LESS) ON JUNE 21, 1997, WITH REBECCA LOBO'S NEW YORK LIBERTY FACING LISA LESLIE'S LOS ANGELES SPARKS IN THE FORUM, HOME OF THE NBA'S LAKERS.

THE ABL ACTUALLY PAID *MORE*, BUT PLAYERS KNEW THAT ASSOCIATION WITH THE NBA WOULD ATTRACT BIGGER MARKETS AND LUCRATIVE CORPORATE SPONSORS.

MOST OF THE WOMEN WERE PLAYING *PROFESSIONALLY* BEFORE FANS AND FRIENDS AND FAMILY IN THEIR HOME COUNTRY FOR THE FIRST TIME *EVER*.

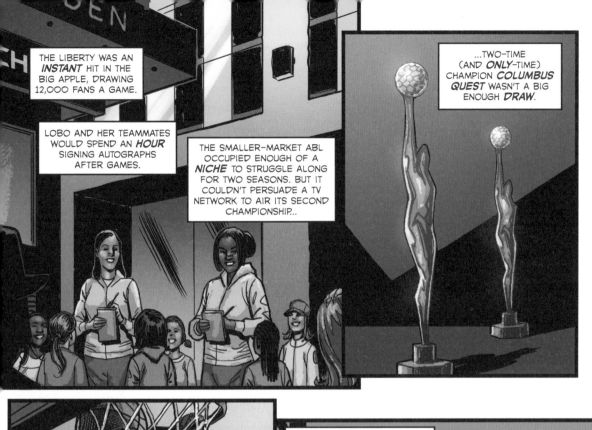

THE LIBERTY WAS AN *INSTANT* HIT IN THE BIG APPLE, DRAWING 12,000 FANS A GAME.

LOBO AND HER TEAMMATES WOULD SPEND AN *HOUR* SIGNING AUTOGRAPHS AFTER GAMES.

THE SMALLER-MARKET ABL OCCUPIED ENOUGH OF A *NICHE* TO STRUGGLE ALONG FOR TWO SEASONS. BUT IT COULDN'T PERSUADE A TV NETWORK TO AIR ITS SECOND CHAMPIONSHIP...

...TWO-TIME (AND *ONLY*-TIME) CHAMPION *COLUMBUS QUEST* WASN'T A BIG ENOUGH *DRAW*.

THE ABL ALL-STAR GAME WAS HELD AT DISNEY WORLD IN ORLANDO AND BOASTED A *BLINDFOLDED DUNK* FROM SYLVIA CRAWLEY THAT WOULD HAVE MADE DR. J PROUD.

THE ABL PLAYED WHAT MOST HOOPS WONKS CONSIDERED A *SUPERIOR* BRAND OF BASKETBALL AND KEPT INCREASING ATTENDANCE, BUT IT WAS SWIMMING *UPSTREAM* AGAINST THE WNBA JUGGERNAUT.

A THIRD-SEASON ADVERTISING PUSH SUCCEEDED ONLY IN SINKING THE ABL DEEPER INTO *DEBT*, AND THE LEAGUE DECLARED BANKRUPTCY ON DECEMBER 22, 1998.

NOW *UNOPPOSED* IN WOMEN'S HOOPS, THE WNBA EXPANDED FROM EIGHT TO SIXTEEN TEAMS OVER THE NEXT TWO YEARS.

BUT THE MAXIMUM WNBA SALARY IS A LITTLE MORE THAN *$100,000* (WHILE THE *MINIMUM* NBA SALARY IS *$838,464*)--AND AMERICAN WOMEN CONTINUE TO PLAY *OVERSEAS* IN THE OFFSEASON TO ENHANCE THEIR EARNING POWER.

WBA 1993 1995

WPBL 1978 1981

ABL 1996 1999

TAKE THE NEW YORK LIBERTY'S DIMINUTIVE (5' 6") POINT GUARD, **BECKY HAMMON**, WHO HAD HER BREAKOUT SEASON IN 2003.

ONE WONDERS IF HER *SIZE* WAS PART OF THE REASON SHE WASN'T INVITED TO TRY OUT FOR THE TEAM USA THAT COMPETED IN THE 2008 OLYMPICS.

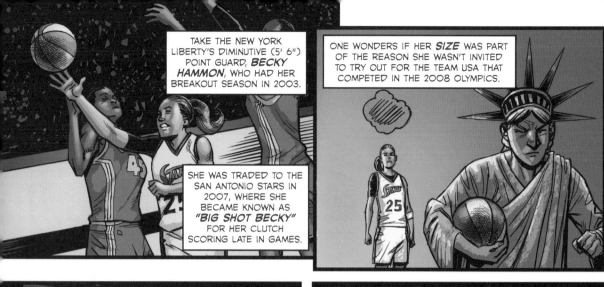

SHE WAS TRADED TO THE SAN ANTONIO STARS IN 2007, WHERE SHE BECAME KNOWN AS *"BIG SHOT BECKY"* FOR HER CLUTCH SCORING LATE IN GAMES.

BUT THE *RUSSIAN* NATIONAL TEAM INVITED HAMMON TO PLAY FOR *THEM*.

THEY EVIDENTLY WANTED TO RECAPTURE SOME OF THE SOVIET UNION'S COLD WAR-ERA HOOPS DOMINANCE BY ASSEMBLING THEIR OWN "DREAM TEAM."

THE ONLY *CATCH* WAS THAT HAMMON HAD TO BECOME A NATURALIZED *RUSSIAN CITIZEN* TO QUALIFY FOR THE TEAM.

IT WASN'T AN EASY DECISION; TEAM USA'S COACH INITIALLY DENOUNCED HER AS *UNPATRIOTIC*.

HER REPUTATION TOOK A BEATING BACK IN HER HOME STATE OF SOUTH DAKOTA, AND FOR A TIME HER MOTHER COULDN'T CALL HER WITHOUT CRYING.

AT BEIJING, TEAM USA ONCE AGAIN WON THE GOLD, BUT BECKY LED RUSSIA TO THE BRONZE, SCORING A TEAM-HIGH 22 POINTS. (AT THE MEDAL CEREMONY, TEAM USA'S LISA LESLIE REFUSED TO SHAKE HER HAND.)

SHE PLAYED FOR THE RUSSIANS AGAIN IN THE 2012 LONDON GAMES. THIS TIME, AUSTRALIA DEFEATED HAMMON'S SQUAD IN THE BRONZE-MEDAL MATCH.

ON HER WAY BACK TO AMERICA, SHE RAN INTO SAN ANTONIO SPURS COACH *GREGG POPOVICH* WHILE MAKING A CONNECTING FLIGHT IN ATLANTA.

POPOVICH IS A LEGEND FOR HIS INNOVATIVE METHODS, NO-NONSENSE ATTITUDE, AND ABILITY TO WIN--HIS SPURS HAVE WON FIVE NBA TITLES AND (AS OF THIS WRITING, HE'S STILL THE COACH) HAD A WINNING RECORD FOR AN UNPRECEDENTED *TWENTY-ONE SEASONS.*

POPOVICH HAD ALSO BEEN A *SOVIET SPECIALIST* IN THE AIR FORCE ACADEMY, AND WAS FASCINATED TO HEAR ABOUT HAMMON'S ADVENTURES IN RUSSIA DURING THE FLIGHT FROM ATLANTA.

HE WAS IMPRESSED BY HER ON-COURT LEADERSHIP.

"I'D WATCH THE GAME, AND THE ONLY THING I COULD SEE WAS BECKY'S *AURA*, HER *LEADERSHIP*, HER EFFECT ON THE CROWD, THE WAY SHE HANDLED HERSELF," HE SAID.

HE ASKED HER WHAT SHE PLANNED TO DO AFTER HER PLAYING CAREER WAS OVER.

IF I EVER *HIRED* YOU AND I ASKED YOU SOMETHING, YOU'D TELL ME THE *TRUTH?*

I DON'T KNOW WHY ELSE YOU'D *ASK* IF YOU DIDN'T WANT ME TO TELL THE *TRUTH.*

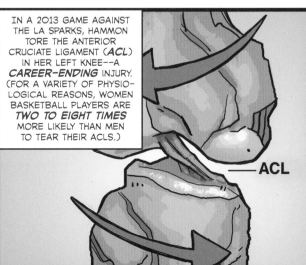

IN A 2013 GAME AGAINST THE LA SPARKS, HAMMON TORE THE ANTERIOR CRUCIATE LIGAMENT (*ACL*) IN HER LEFT KNEE--A *CAREER-ENDING* INJURY. (FOR A VARIETY OF PHYSIO-LOGICAL REASONS, WOMEN BASKETBALL PLAYERS ARE *TWO TO EIGHT TIMES* MORE LIKELY THAN MEN TO TEAR THEIR ACLS.)

—ACL

HAMMON SPENT A YEAR RECOVERING FROM HER INJURY. TO THE SURPRISE OF MANY, THE FAMOUSLY SECRETIVE POPOVICH ALLOWED BECKY TO WATCH SPURS' *PRACTICES* FROM THE SIDELINES.

IN THE SUMMER OF 2014, HAMMON FORMALLY RETIRED FROM THE WNBA--AND POPOVICH HIRED HER AS A FULL-TIME *ASSISTANT COACH*, THE FIRST WOMAN TO COACH MALE PROS IN AMERICAN SPORTS HISTORY.

IT HAS NOTHING TO DO WITH HER BEING A WOMAN. SHE *HAPPENS* TO BE A WOMAN.

MEN, OF COURSE, HAVE COACHED *WOMEN* SINCE THE GAME'S BEGINNING, BUT THE CONVENTIONAL WISDOM HAS ALWAYS BEEN THAT MACHO ATHLETES WOULD BALK AT *TAKING ORDERS* FROM A LADY-PERSON.

SSH! HIDE AND MAYBE SHE'LL GO AWAY!

PREDICTABLY, CERTAIN CORNERS OF THE INTERNET DENOUNCED THE MOVE AS A PUBLICITY STUNT--TROLLS CLAIMED THAT THE ONLY THING HAMMON COULD TEACH THE SPURS WAS HOW TO *BAKE COOKIES.*

UNFAZED, HAMMON TACKLED HER NEW ROLE WITH THE SAME DISINTEREST IN OTHER PEOPLE'S OPINIONS THAT ALLOWED HER TO PLAY FOR THE RUSSIANS, AND SHE QUICKLY GAINED THE RESPECT OF THE SPURS PLAYERS WITH HER BASKETBALL INTELLIGENCE.

MURRAY 5

(CONVENTIONAL WISDOM PERHAPS SHOULD HAVE CONSIDERED THAT MACHO ATHLETES AREN'T *INSECURE ENOUGH* TO BALK AT FOLLOWING A WOMAN.)

NBA ASSISTANT COACHES TYPICALLY TAKE LEAD DURING THE SUMMER LEAGUE IN LAS VEGAS. IN 2015, BECKY HAMMON BECAME THE SAN ANTONIO SPURS' OFFSEASON HEAD COACH...

...AND BECAME THE FIRST *FEMALE* COACH TO LEAD HER *ALL-MALE* TEAM TO A *CHAMPIONSHIP.*

WHAT IF, IN THE FUTURE, A WOMAN *WINS* THE NBA CROWN...

...NOT AS A PLAYER, BUT AS A *COACH?*

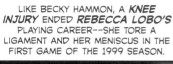

LIKE BECKY HAMMON, A **KNEE INJURY** ENDED **REBECCA LOBO'S** PLAYING CAREER--SHE TORE A LIGAMENT AND HER MENISCUS IN THE FIRST GAME OF THE 1999 SEASON.

SHE WAS SELECTED FOR THE FIRST WNBA ALL-STAR TEAM BUT HAD TO WATCH FROM THE BENCH.

ULTIMATELY, HER KNEE ISSUES WOULD FORCE AN EARLY RETIREMENT IN 2003.

LIKE SO MANY FORMER PLAYERS, WHEN SHE SET DOWN A BALL, SHE PICKED UP A MICROPHONE, SPENDING FIFTEEN YEARS COVERING COLLEGE BALL AND THE WNBA FOR ESPN.

REBECCA LOBO WAS INDUCTED INTO THE NAISMITH BASKETBALL HALL OF FAME IN 2017. THE HALL AND MUSEUM ARE IN SPRINGFIELD, MASSACHUSETTS, WHERE THE GAME WAS **BORN**, NOT FAR FROM WHERE LOBO GREW UP IN SOUTHWICK.

THE AUDIENCE AT SPRINGFIELD SYMPHONY HALL GAVE THEIR HOMETOWN HERO A MASSIVE **OVATION** AS SHE STRODE TO THE STAGE.

IN HER ACCEPTANCE SPEECH, SHE TOLD A STORY ABOUT HOW FAR THE WOMEN'S GAME HAD COME.

HER FOUR-AND-A-HALF-YEAR-OLD DAUGHTER WAS WATCHING A UCONN MEN'S BASKETBALL GAME ON TV WITH HER PARENTS, AND SAID:

ARE THOSE BOYS PLAYING?

YES.

I DIDN'T KNOW **BOYS** PLAYED BASKETBALL!

CHAPTER ELEVEN
THE GAME OF THE NOW

ON JULY 8, 2010, A HIGHLY *UNUSUAL* BROADCAST APPEARED ON ESPN.

GREAT FUTURES START HERE.

BOYS & GIRLS CLUBS

ENTITLED "THE DECISION," IT FEATURED UNRESTRICTED FREE AGENT *LEBRON JAMES*, WHO WAS GOING TO USE IT TO ANNOUNCE WHICH TEAM HE WOULD SIGN WITH.

JAMES HAD SPENT HIS ENTIRE NBA CAREER TO THAT POINT WITH HIS HOMETOWN *CLEVELAND CAVALIERS.*

BORN AND GROWING UP IN NEARBY AKRON, OHIO, JAMES WOULD *STARE* AT THE MAPS OF THE USA HANGING IN HIS SCHOOL CLASSROOMS AND WONDER WHY HIS CITY WASN'T *ON* THEM.

HIS MOTHER, GLORIA MARIE, WAS *SIXTEEN* WHEN HE WAS BORN, AND YOUNG LEBRON DIDN'T KNOW WHO HIS BIOLOGICAL FATHER WAS. THE MAN HE CALLED "DAD" WAS OFTEN IN PRISON.

AKRON, A FORMER RUBBER CAPITAL, NOW EPITOMIZED RUST-BELT WASTELAND.

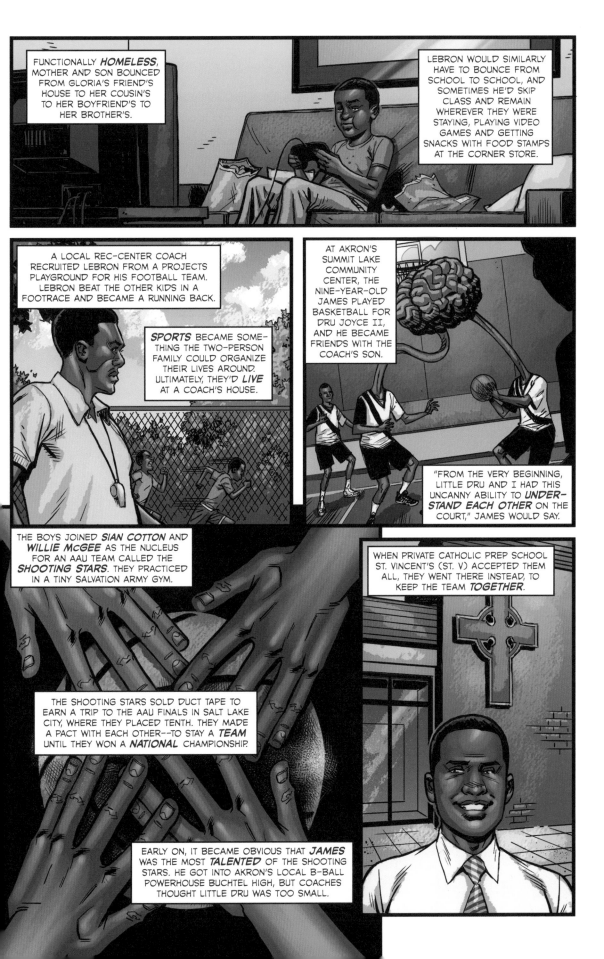

FUNCTIONALLY *HOMELESS*, MOTHER AND SON BOUNCED FROM GLORIA'S FRIEND'S HOUSE TO HER COUSIN'S TO HER BOYFRIEND'S TO HER BROTHER'S.

LEBRON WOULD SIMILARLY HAVE TO BOUNCE FROM SCHOOL TO SCHOOL, AND SOMETIMES HE'D SKIP CLASS AND REMAIN WHEREVER THEY WERE STAYING, PLAYING VIDEO GAMES AND GETTING SNACKS WITH FOOD STAMPS AT THE CORNER STORE.

A LOCAL REC-CENTER COACH RECRUITED LEBRON FROM A PROJECTS PLAYGROUND FOR HIS FOOTBALL TEAM. LEBRON BEAT THE OTHER KIDS IN A FOOTRACE AND BECAME A RUNNING BACK.

AT AKRON'S SUMMIT LAKE COMMUNITY CENTER, THE NINE-YEAR-OLD JAMES PLAYED BASKETBALL FOR DRU JOYCE II, AND HE BECAME FRIENDS WITH THE COACH'S SON.

SPORTS BECAME SOME-THING THE TWO-PERSON FAMILY COULD ORGANIZE THEIR LIVES AROUND. ULTIMATELY, THEY'D *LIVE* AT A COACH'S HOUSE.

"FROM THE VERY BEGINNING, LITTLE DRU AND I HAD THIS UNCANNY ABILITY TO *UNDER-STAND EACH OTHER* ON THE COURT," JAMES WOULD SAY.

THE BOYS JOINED *SIAN COTTON* AND *WILLIE McGEE* AS THE NUCLEUS FOR AN AAU TEAM CALLED THE *SHOOTING STARS*. THEY PRACTICED IN A TINY SALVATION ARMY GYM.

WHEN PRIVATE CATHOLIC PREP SCHOOL ST. VINCENT'S (ST. V) ACCEPTED THEM ALL, THEY WENT THERE INSTEAD, TO KEEP THE TEAM *TOGETHER*.

THE SHOOTING STARS SOLD DUCT TAPE TO EARN A TRIP TO THE AAU FINALS IN SALT LAKE CITY, WHERE THEY PLACED TENTH. THEY MADE A PACT WITH EACH OTHER--TO STAY A *TEAM* UNTIL THEY WON A *NATIONAL* CHAMPIONSHIP.

EARLY ON, IT BECAME OBVIOUS THAT *JAMES* WAS THE MOST *TALENTED* OF THE SHOOTING STARS. HE GOT INTO AKRON'S LOCAL B-BALL POWERHOUSE BUCHTEL HIGH, BUT COACHES THOUGHT LITTLE DRU WAS TOO SMALL.

UNLIKE BUCHTEL, ST. V WAS ALMOST ENTIRELY *WHITE*. WHEN COACH DRU GOT A JOB THERE, HE AND HIS BOYS WERE ACCUSED OF *SELLING OUT* BY MANY IN THE BLACK COMMUNITY.

I HEAR YOU'RE PIMPING FOR ST. V!

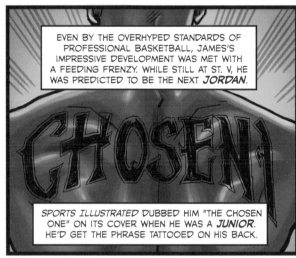

EVEN BY THE OVERHYPED STANDARDS OF PROFESSIONAL BASKETBALL, JAMES'S IMPRESSIVE DEVELOPMENT WAS MET WITH A FEEDING FRENZY. WHILE STILL AT ST. V, HE WAS PREDICTED TO BE THE NEXT *JORDAN*.

CHOSEN

SPORTS ILLUSTRATED DUBBED HIM "THE CHOSEN ONE" ON ITS COVER WHEN HE WAS A *JUNIOR*. HE'D GET THE PHRASE TATTOOED ON HIS BACK.

JAMES WAS SUCH A *SOUGHT-AFTER* PLAYER THAT REPORTERS STARTED FOLLOWING HIM AROUND AT SCHOOL, TO THE POINT WHERE ST. V'S PRINCIPAL HAD TO BAN THEM.

THESE GUYS NEED TO GET A *LIFE*, AND I'M NOT IT!

PROGRAMS WITH HIS SIGNATURE WOULD WIND UP ON *EBAY* FOR VAST SUMS. SCALPERS SOLD TICKETS TO THEIR GAMES AT VASTLY *INFLATED* PRICES.

HIS MOTHER BOUGHT HIM A *HUMMER H2* FOR HIS EIGHTEENTH BIRTHDAY WITH A LOAN AGAINST HIS FUTURE NBA EARNINGS, PROMPTING AN INVESTIGATION BY THE OHIO HIGH SCHOOL ATHLETIC ASSOCIATION.

WHEN AN ADMIRING CLOTHING-STORE CLERK GAVE LEBRON TWO JERSEYS FOR FREE, JAMES WAS *SUSPENDED* FOR THE BULK OF THE SEASON FOR "UNSPORTSMANLIKE BEHAVIOR."

THE *COURTS* REINSTATED HIM JUST IN TIME FOR THE PLAYOFFS. IN THE NATIONAL CHAMPIONSHIP, ST. V DEFEATED KETTERING ARCHBISHOP ALTER, 40-36.

EVEN THEN, THE BOYS KNEW THAT THE BOND BETWEEN THEM WOULD *SLIP AWAY*, AS LEBRON PREPARED, LIKE KOBE BRYANT BEFORE HIM, TO GO STRAIGHT FROM HIGH SCHOOL TO THE NBA DRAFT.

IN HIS 2002-03 ROOKIE SEASON WITH CLEVELAND, JAMES AVERAGED 20.9 POINTS AND 5.9 ASSISTS, THE FIRST CAV AND JUST THE THIRD NBA PLAYER OVERALL TO DO SO.

THE NEXT YEAR HE SET CLEVELAND'S SINGLE-GAME SCORING RECORD (56) AGAINST TORONTO.

IN GAME 5 OF THE 2007 NBA CONFERENCE FINALS, JAMES CAPPED HIS 48-POINT PERFORMANCE (SCORING 29 OF THE CAVS' LAST 30) WITH A GAME-WINNING LAYUP AGAINST THE PISTONS WITH TWO SECONDS TO SPARE.

CLEVELAND *LOVED* HER HOMEGROWN HERO, AND HIS PREGAME TOSS OF CRUSHED CHALK INTO THE AIR BECAME THE STUFF OF LEGEND.

IN 2009, JAMES BECAME THE FIRST CAVALIER TO WIN THE MVP AWARD, AND HE WON IT AGAIN IN 2010-- HIS FREE-AGENCY YEAR.

LEBRON TOURED SIX CITIES THAT WENT OUT OF THEIR WAY TO COURT HIM.

SO WHEN, IN THE CLIMAX OF "THE DECISION," HE ANNOUNCED,

THIS FALL I'M GOING TO TAKE MY TALENTS TO *SOUTH BEACH* AND JOIN THE *MIAMI HEAT...*

...FANS IN OHIO, WELL, THEY DIDN'T *TAKE IT TOO WELL.*

"KING JAMES" JERSEYS WERE TREATED LIKE *WITCHES IN SALEM.*

As you now know, our former hero, who grew up in the very region that he deserted this evening, is no longer a Cleveland Cavalier.

This was announced with a several day, narcissistic, self-promotional build-up culminating with a national TV special of his "decision" unlike anything ever "witnessed" in the history of sports and probably the history of entertainment.

Clearly, this is bitterly disappointing to all of us.

CRITICS OUTSIDE MIAMI COMPLAINED THAT IT SMACKED OF *COLLUSION*--THAT LEBRON AND FELLOW FREE AGENT CHRIS BOSH *CONSPIRED* WITH MIAMI STAR DWYANE WADE TO CREATE A *SUPER-TEAM* THAT WOULD GUARANTEE THE CHAMPIONSHIP THAT JAMES CRAVED--AND HE DIDN'T SEE HAPPENING IN CLEVELAND.

FEW SPORTS ARE AS SUSCEPTIBLE TO THIS KIND OF *MANIPULATION* AS BASKETBALL--EVER SINCE THE MINNESOTA LAKERS *"WAITED FOR MIKAN,"* THE GAME HAS BEEN DOMINATED BY A HANDFUL OF *"BIG MEN."*

FOR MANY, "THE DECISION" EMBODIED ALL THE PROBLEMS OF MODERN BASKETBALL...

...IN WHICH SELFISH MILLIONAIRE PLAYERS WAR ENDLESSLY WITH *MULTI-MILLIONAIRE* OWNERS WITH NO CARE FOR THE *FANS* WHO FOOT THE BILL FOR THEIR SALARIES.

THEY BATTLE WITH EACH OTHER ON *SOCIAL MEDIA* MORE FIERCELY THAN ON THE COURT--OR AT LEAST UNTIL THE OVERLONG *POSTSEASON* STARTS.

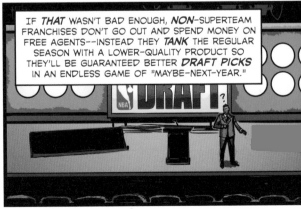

IF *THAT* WASN'T BAD ENOUGH, *NON*-SUPERTEAM FRANCHISES DON'T GO OUT AND SPEND MONEY ON FREE AGENTS--INSTEAD THEY *TANK* THE REGULAR SEASON WITH A LOWER-QUALITY PRODUCT SO THEY'LL BE GUARANTEED BETTER *DRAFT PICKS* IN AN ENDLESS GAME OF "MAYBE-NEXT-YEAR."

EVEN WITH ALL OF THOSE ISSUES, THOUGH, BASKETBALL CURRENTLY ENJOYS *UNPRECEDENTED* POPULARITY.

THE WRITING OF THIS BOOK WAS MOSTLY COMPLETED DURING THE ALL-STAR GAME BREAK OF THE 2018-19 NBA SEASON.

THE LEAGUE'S TELEVISION RATINGS WERE UP 32 PERCENT THE PREVIOUS YEAR, AND IN-PERSON ATTENDANCE GREW FOR A RECORD-SETTING FOURTH CONSECUTIVE YEAR.

INCREDIBLY, THE SPORT'S SOCIAL CONSCIOUSNESS HAS *INCREASED* RATHER THAN BEEN *DIMINISHED* DURING ITS ASCENDANCE.

PREVIOUS GENERATIONS' DESIRE FOR SPORTS TO BE *APOLITICAL* HAS BEEN THROWN OUT THE WINDOW. BASKETBALL PLAYERS SPEAK OUT AGAINST SOCIAL INJUSTICE MORE THAN EVER BEFORE.

ON APRIL 24, 2014, THE OWNER OF THE LA CLIPPERS, *DONALD STERLING,* WAS CAUGHT ON TAPE TELLING HIS GIRLFRIEND HE DIDN'T WANT TO SEE HER BRINGING BLACK PEOPLE TO GAMES.

NEW COMMISSIONER ADAM SILVER *BANNED* STERLING FOR LIFE TWO DAYS AFTER THE RECORDING LEAKED, AND THE CLIPPERS WERE QUICKLY SOLD.

IN AMERICA, WHERE WHITE RICH GUYS STILL OWN TEAMS POPULATED PRIMARILY BY BLACK PLAYERS WHO GREW UP POOR, IT WAS INCONCEIVABLE THAT ANY *OTHER* SPORT WOULD HAVE REACTED SO QUICKLY.

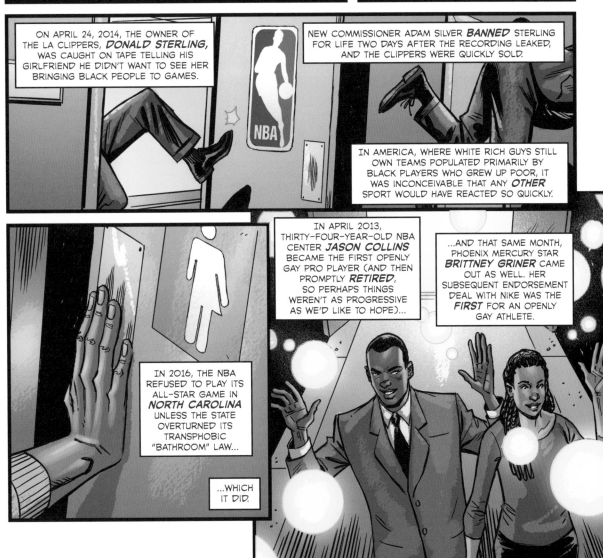

IN APRIL 2013, THIRTY-FOUR-YEAR-OLD NBA CENTER *JASON COLLINS* BECAME THE FIRST OPENLY GAY PRO PLAYER (AND THEN PROMPTLY *RETIRED,* SO PERHAPS THINGS WEREN'T AS PROGRESSIVE AS WE'D LIKE TO HOPE)...

...AND THAT SAME MONTH, PHOENIX MERCURY STAR *BRITTNEY GRINER* CAME OUT AS WELL. HER SUBSEQUENT ENDORSEMENT DEAL WITH NIKE WAS THE *FIRST* FOR AN OPENLY GAY ATHLETE.

IN 2016, THE NBA REFUSED TO PLAY ITS ALL-STAR GAME IN *NORTH CAROLINA* UNLESS THE STATE OVERTURNED ITS TRANSPHOBIC "BATHROOM" LAW...

...WHICH IT DID.

THE STORY OF BASKETBALL *CONTINUES*, WITH MANY CHAPTERS STILL *UNFINISHED*.

IN 2012, A WORLDWIDE OUTBREAK OF *"LINSANITY"* ACCOMPANIED THE ASTOUNDING SCORING RUN OF KNICKS POINT GUARD *JEREMY LIN*, THE FIRST AMERICAN-BORN CHINESE PLAYER IN THE NBA.

AFTER A FEW QUIET PRO SEASONS, HE SUDDENLY BROKE OUT AS AN OFFENSIVE SENSATION IN A SERIES OF SPECTACULAR PERFORMANCES.

TIM DUNCAN BECAME THE GREATEST *POWER FORWARD* OF ALL TIME WITH THE SAN ANTONIO SPURS, AND THE *OLDEST* PLAYER TO HAVE A 20-20 GAME EVER, WITH 23 POINTS AND 21 REBOUNDS AGAINST THE ATLANTA HAWKS ON DECEMBER 2, 2013.

WHEN HE RETIRED IN 2016, THE FIFTEEN-TIME NBA ALL-STAR WAS THE ONLY PLAYER TO BE SELECTED TO BOTH THE ALL-NBA AND ALL-DEFENSIVE TEAMS FOR THIRTEEN CONSECUTIVE SEASONS.

THE *GOLDEN STATE WARRIORS* EMBARKED ON A CHAMPIONSHIP DYNASTY (THREE CROWNS AND COUNTING AS OF THIS WRITING) WITH THE BEST SHOOTING TEAM IN LEAGUE HISTORY, NEARLY IMPOSSIBLE TO GUARD.

LED BY SUPERLATIVE POINT GUARD *STEPH CURRY*, THEY ARE THE FIRST TEAM IN HISTORY TO WIN AT LEAST SIXTY-SEVEN GAMES THREE SEASONS IN A ROW.

AFTER WINNING TWO CHAMPIONSHIPS IN MIAMI, LEBRON JAMES *RETURNED* TO THE CAVALIERS AND ENDED CLEVELAND'S DECADES-LONG CHAMPIONSHIP DROUGHT BY LEADING THE CAVS TO THE 2016 NBA CROWN.

NORTHEAST OHIO WELCOMED BACK ITS PRODIGAL SON AND DIDN'T EVEN SEEM ALL THAT NONPLUSSED WHEN HE LEFT *ONCE MORE* TO JOIN THE LAKERS FOR THE 2018-19 SEASON.

IN RETROSPECT, IT SEEMS A *LITTLE* UNFAIR TO BLAME LEBRON FOR "THE DECISION."

CLEVELAND

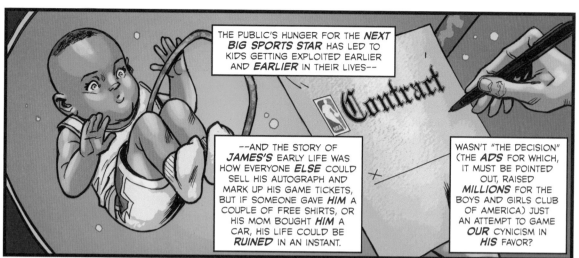

THE PUBLIC'S HUNGER FOR THE **NEXT BIG SPORTS STAR** HAS LED TO KIDS GETTING EXPLOITED EARLIER AND **EARLIER** IN THEIR LIVES--

--AND THE STORY OF **JAMES'S** EARLY LIFE WAS HOW EVERYONE **ELSE** COULD SELL HIS AUTOGRAPH AND MARK UP HIS GAME TICKETS, BUT IF SOMEONE GAVE **HIM** A COUPLE OF FREE SHIRTS, OR HIS MOM BOUGHT **HIM** A CAR, HIS LIFE COULD BE **RUINED** IN AN INSTANT.

WASN'T "THE DECISION" (THE **ADS** FOR WHICH, IT MUST BE POINTED OUT, RAISED **MILLIONS** FOR THE BOYS AND GIRLS CLUB OF AMERICA) JUST AN ATTEMPT TO GAME **OUR** CYNICISM IN **HIS** FAVOR?

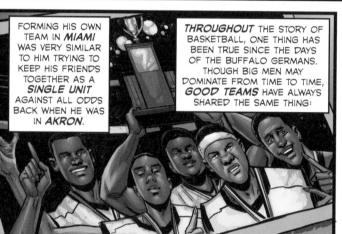

FORMING HIS OWN TEAM IN **MIAMI** WAS VERY SIMILAR TO HIM TRYING TO KEEP HIS FRIENDS TOGETHER AS A **SINGLE UNIT** AGAINST ALL ODDS BACK WHEN HE WAS IN **AKRON.**

THROUGHOUT THE STORY OF BASKETBALL, ONE THING HAS BEEN TRUE SINCE THE DAYS OF THE BUFFALO GERMANS. THOUGH BIG MEN MAY DOMINATE FROM TIME TO TIME, **GOOD TEAMS** HAVE ALWAYS SHARED THE SAME THING:

"THE **SECRET** OF BASKETBALL," ISIAH THOMAS ONCE TOLD SPORTSWRITER BILL SIMMONS, "IS THAT IT'S NOT **ABOUT** BASKETBALL."

HIS PISTONS WON "BECAUSE THEY LIKED EACH OTHER, KNEW THEIR ROLES, IGNORED STATIS-TICS, AND VALUED **WINNING** OVER EVERYTHING ELSE."

EASY AND FREE PLAY, UNHINDERED BY SELF.

THIS IS WHAT MAKES B-BALL LOVED BY WHEELCHAIR-BOUND **PARALYMPIANS...**

...AND THE SILVER-HAIRED PLAYERS OF THE **NATIONAL SENIOR WOMEN'S BASKETBALL ASSOCIATION.**

YOUNG, OLD, OF ANY RACE AND EVERY NATION--THE UNBROKEN HOOP OF BASKETBALL CONNECTS THEM **ALL.**

INDEX

Library of Congress Control Number: 2020935069

Trade Paperback ISBN: 978-1-9848-5618-0
eBook ISBN: 978-1-9848-5619-7

Printed in South Korea

Design by Chloe Rawlins
Color by Dave Swartz
Lettering by Fred Van Lente

10 9 8 7 6 5 4 3 2 1

First Edition